IMAGINE: Believe, See and Achieve Your Destiny

Thank you for your generous gift
Love Barbie

Presented to

Kathliene Sundt

From

Dr Barbie L Breathitt

Date

December 2020

DecodeMyDream.com

The FREE Dream Journal at **DecodeMyDream.com** gives you the opportunity to record and preserve your dreams. Then submit them to our dream analysis specialists for an in-depth and biblically sound analysis.

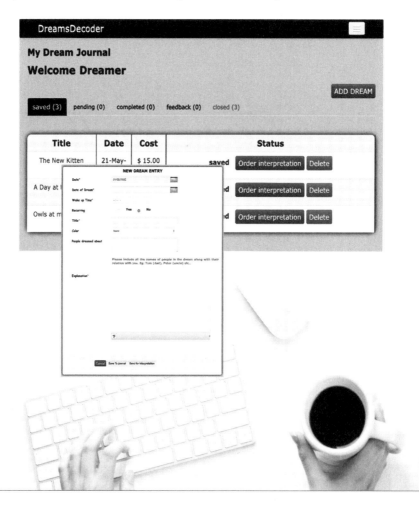

PROPHETIC LIFE DREAM COACH

ASK BARBIE

PRIVATE, HOUR-LONG PHONE SESSIONS
EMAIL INFO@BARBIEBREATHITT.COM
CALL 972-253-6653

ASKBARBIE.COM

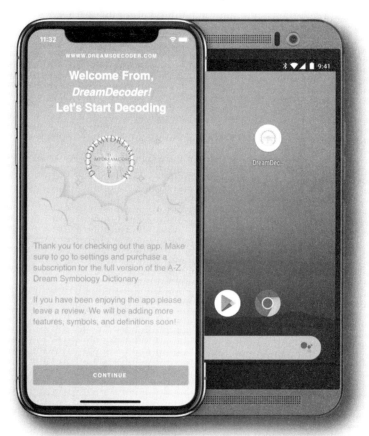

Endorsements

In my most recent book published by Charisma House, *The Passover Prophecies: How God is Realigning Hearts and Nations in Crisis*, I wrote, "We must be a people of imagination like the early pioneers of nations. Isaiah 26 is wonderfully translated in the Passion Translation Bible. I love the way verse 3 is phrased: *those whose imaginations are consumed with you* (Isa. 26:3). The Hebrew word translated "imagination" is *yester*, meaning "form, concept, framework, imagination, mind". A human imagination wholly owned by the Holy Spirit is one of the most powerful redemptive forces on earth.

These times call for a critical, God-filled imagination. This will create a new framework and conceptualization of all the problems around us. Our minds should be fixed on and become consumed by Him. This is what will unleash the supernatural creativity resident in all of the redeemed and will give birth to the exploits necessary for our triumph. In this season, we must reform our minds and imaginations. We must gather raw materials, then shape them into form and identify our future. Our concepts, frameworks, minds and imaginations must unlock into new forms and identities to meet and triumph in the era ahead.

Dr. Barbie Breathitt's five book series, *IMAGINE*, has captured the essence of God's plans to reinvent the church in the fullness of Christ's creative, life-giving, resurrection power with signs and wonders following. Each individual believer must take on his or her Christlike identity as a Son of God to move forward into this era, as One New Man arises to demonstrate God's glory on earth as it is in heaven!

Dr. Chuck D. Pierce
President, Glory of Zion International Ministries
President, Global Spheres in Corinth, Texas

God's ways are higher than our ways, and yet we are invited to co-labor with Christ as partakers in His divine nature. Pioneering ideas in her new book series *IMAGINE*, will open you up to your limitless potential. You will come to know that God created you to navigate life with the mind of Christ, and by faith, you can tap into a Spirit-inspired, creative process that is aligned with God's heart.

Dr. Breathitt's books will help you to understand your call to walk in a prophetic relationship with Jesus and to unlock the powerful truths available to all who believe in Him. This is a fresh invitation to imagine with God, to dream with Him for the future and to access and implement heaven's answers to the world's problems to advance God's Kingdom.

Dr. Ché Ahn
Founder and President, Harvest International Ministry
Founding and Senior Pastor, HROCK Church, Pasadena, CA
International Chancellor, Wagner University
Founder, Ché Ahn Ministries

Many copy or imitate others. Some create a model for others to learn from, and some are innovative. But few are innovators. Others learn a subject matter, then reach a peak and just plain plateau and cease advancing. Then there are those who become constant learners as a lifestyle, filling their heart and soul with the creative realms of God. Dr. Barbie Breathitt is cut from this type of creative fabric.

As an educator and prophetic interpreter/analyst, this consecrated woman of God consistently takes us on an exciting journey of discovery. Can you imagine that? As you partake of Barbie's teachings and her adventurous spirit carved from the boundaries of the Word of God, you, too, will grow in your prophetic imagination into a place where dreams really do come true!

Dr. James W Goll
Founder, God Encounters Ministries and GOLL Ideation LLC
Life Language Communications Coach

Dr. Barbie L. Breathitt is on the cutting edge of using her God-appointed seer gifting to help people gain an enhanced understanding of how God created and operates through the imagination, so that His people can apprehend the mysteries and purposes of God and manifest His glory in the earthly realm."

Cindy Jacobs
Generals International, Dallas, Texas

Beautiful, wonderful and full of divine insight! *IMAGINE* provides the 'missing link' in Christian understanding and practice between the natural and the supernatural realms that many believers have been seeking for years. Dr. Barbie Breathitt has done the body of Christ a great service by providing a solid biblical foundation for understanding how the natural and spiritual interact—how we integrate that process into our own lives by cooperating with the Holy Spirit.

These books are both paradigm-changing and life-altering. It is a wonderful blend of contemplative and analytical biblical thinking, personal experience building and divine revelation that will provide earnest believers with a new blueprint for the kind of walk with God they have always yearned for.

I suggest you read these books slowly and thoughtfully, perhaps several times, because it redefines the normative Christian experience in many fundamental ways. As you train your senses (Hebrews 5:14) this way, you will find yourself thinking all things have become new for me now.

Joan Hunter
Author/Healing Evangelist
Host, TV Show *Miracles Happen*

Dr. Barbie Breathitt's book series *IMAGINE* is a timely message, as this is the hour that God is releasing creative thinking and solutions from heaven. These books will open doorways to anointed thinking and the ability to see in the Spirit. This will activate your ability to dream and create at new levels through the Holy Spirit. This series is grounded in sound biblical teaching and practical instructions of how to apply it to your daily life. It is not just for creative dreamers, seers or songwriters—it is applicable to all the gifts, especially in business and ministry.

Doug Addison
Doug Addison.com
Author, webcast *Hearing God Everyday*, podcast *Daily Prophetic Words*, and prophetic blog *Spirit Connection*

Perfect, absolute peace surrounds those whose imaginations are consumed with you (Isaiah 26:3 TPT). Our imagination enables us to envision the Invisible One and thereby, as Barbie wrote, '…to redesign the image of ourselves.' The imagination is uncharted territory for Christians. We need more people like Dr. Breathitt to lead the way.

Ron Campbell
DreamsDecoder.com

In her *IMAGINE* series, Dr. Barbie Breathitt's intensity of personae invites readers to partake in her deep insights, advanced levels of understanding and supernatural operations of faith in the glory realm. She challenges us not only to dream but also dares us to courageously imagine the impossible. Barbie creatively inspires us to unlock our potential in Christ through our imagination, to transcend the limitations of the flesh and progress in the limitless dimensions of God's glory.

I was often labeled as and teased about being a fantasizer during my childhood years, which greatly stifled the use of my imagination. The *IMAGINE* series has now unlocked the door to my imaginativeness, allowing me to freely and confidently advance. I have been awakened to the vast dimensions of God consciousness and His power, which equip me to exist and operate far beyond my God-given anointings and giftings. This series empowers me to live my future in the now!

Michael Adeyemi Adefarasin
Kingdom Lifeline Apostolic Ministries (KLAM), Abuja, Nigeria

A new era has dawned for God's people! A newfound season of supernatural revelation is being released from heaven to those who have the spiritual eyes and ears to see and hear what the Spirit is doing and saying (see Revelation 3:22).

Dr. Barbie Breathitt's *IMAGINE* series issues a clarion call for Believers to arise and supplant the old nature and attain their new identity in Christ. She implores readers to take on the very nature of Christ. She encourages them to utilize their divine imagination to create and decree their God-purposed destinies into reality in the same way God imagined and created before the beginning of time. Readers will discover the fundamental knowledge of how to apply their infinite imagination to shape their individual lives, influence the world and execute God's purposes.

Allow Barbie's *IMAGINE* series to transform your mind and usher you into a higher dimension of the Lord's destiny for your life!

Barbara Wentroble
President, International Breakthrough Ministries (IbM)
President, Breakthrough Business Leaders (BBL)
Author, Releasing the Voice of the Ekklesia; Becoming a Wealth Creator; Council Room of the Lord (series)

IMAGINE: Believe, See and Achieve Your Destiny

Works by the Author

Angels in God's Kingdom

Dream Encounters: Seeing Your Destiny from God's Perspective

Gateway to the Seer Realm: Look Again to See Beyond the Natural

So You Want to Change the World?

Hearing and Understanding the Voice of God

Dream Seer: Searching for the Face of the Invisible

Dream Interpreter

A to Z Dream Symbology Dictionary

Volume I Dream Symbols

Volume II Dream Symbols

Volume III Dream Symbols

Action Dream Symbols

When Will My Dreams Come True?

Dream Sexology

Sports & Recreation Dream Symbols

DreamsDecoder.com

IMAGINE
BELIEVE, SEE AND ACHIEVE YOUR DESTINY

Dr. Barbie Breathitt
VOLUME 5

IMAGINE: Believe, See and Achieve Your Destiny

© Copyright 2020–Barbie Breathitt Enterprises All rights reserved.

This book is protected by the copyright laws of the United States of America. This book may not be copied or reprinted for commercial gain or profit. The use of short quotations or occasional page copying for personal or group study is permitted and encouraged. Permission will be granted upon request. Unless otherwise identified, Scripture quotations are taken from the NEW AMERICAN STANDARD BIBLE®, Copyright©1960, 1962, 1963,1968,1971,1972,1973, 1975,1977,1995 by The Lockman Foundation. Used by permission. Scripture quotations marked NKJV are taken from the New King James Version. Copyright © 1982 by Thomas Nelson, Inc. Used by permission. All rights reserved. Scripture quotations marked NIV are taken from the HOLY BIBLE, NEW INTERNATIONAL VERSION®, Copyright © 1973, 1978, 1984 International Bible Society. Used by permission of Zondervan. All rights reserved. Scripture quotations marked MSG are taken from The Message. Copyright © 1993, 1994, 1995, 1996, 2000, 2001, 2002. Used by permission of NavPress Publishing Group. Scripture quotations marked AMP are taken from the Amplified® Bible, Copyright © 1954, 1958, 1962, 1964, 1965, 1987 by The Lockman Foundation. Used by permission. Scripture quotations marked NLT are taken from the Holy Bible, New Living Translation, copyright 1996, 2004. Used by permission of Tyndale House Publishers., Wheaton, Illinois 60189. All rights reserved. Scripture quotations marked KJV are taken from the King James Version. Scripture quotations marked CJB are taken from the Complete Jewish Bible, copyright ©1998 by David H. Stern. Published by Jewish New Testament Publications, Inc. www.messianicjewish.net/jntp. Distributed by Messianic Jewish Resources Int'l. www.messianicjewish.net. All rights reserved. Used by permission. Scripture quotations marked ERV are taken from the Easy to- Read Version Copyright ©2006 World Bible Translation Center. Used by permission. All rights reserved.

All rights reserved. No part of this publication may be reproduced, stored in a retrieval system, or transmitted in any form or by any means, electronic, mechanical, photocopying, recording, or otherwise, without the prior written permission of the publisher.

Breath of the Spirit Ministries, Inc.
P.O. Box 1356
Lake Dallas, Texas 75065
BarbieBreathitt.com
BarbieBreathittEnterprises.com
DreamsDecoder.com

ISBN-13: 978-1-942551-09-6

Published by: Barbie Breathitt Enterprises, Inc.

Printed in Canada.

Dedication

It is my deepest honor to dedicate my series of five *IMAGINE* books to my best friend, personal confidant and beautiful baby sister, Brenda Doreen Breathitt. She was born in Lakeland, Florida on October 29, 1966 and transitioned into Heaven on Saturday, September 7, 2019 at the age of fifty-two. Brenda was a brilliant light of joy with an excellent sense of humor that caused us all to laugh. Her warm, inviting smile disarmed people, letting them know she was a safe place to share their hearts. Brenda was clothed with grace, compassion and beauty that sprang up from a deep well within her loving heart. Her caring concern for others exuded from her countenance to bless all those who knew her. Brenda was full of godly strength and dignity.

Brenda's name meant *the glory of God's sword. Let all who seek You rejoice and be glad in You; and let those who love Your salvation say continually, let God be magnified* (Psalm 70:4). She laughed and loved well through her painful battle with cancer knowing in the days to come she had a home in heaven. Her thoughts and prayers were with her unsaved friends and family members that she was leaving behind. She spoke with wisdom and godly counsel always carrying faithful instruction on her tongue. She diligently watched over her family, friends and household never eating the bread of idleness. Her only daughter Chelsea arises to call her blessed. There are many women who do noble things, but Brenda's loving nature, quick wit, sterling character and integrity surpassed them all. We all know that charm is deceptive, and physical beauty is fleeting; but I praise Brenda for she was a woman who feared the Lord. Those who had the chance to know Brenda honor her memory for all that her hands have done. No matter where Brenda went she always found a friend. Her sweet words of comfort bring her praise from the city gates. Brenda blessed so many in her life with unconditional love, a listening ear, and words of encouragement, profound humor and a shared smile. Brenda made all of us better people for having known her. She is sorely missed.

Barbie

Thank You

A special thank you to heaven's Prophetic Poet Keat Wade for sharing the amazing poems he has authored in his four amazing books: *For Whom Beyond Beckons, Dueling Kingdoms: Chronicling the Times, A Gnarled Tree and Me,* and *Chronology of Love: Times and Seasons.* All of his incredible poems are available on Amazon.com and through Christian Publishing Xulon Press.

Keat Wade's poems are unique in three ways, (1) the supernatural way poems are received (2) the visual of what is going on in the supernatural realm (3) and being in sync with God's Timing (Hebrew Calendar). Keat Wade shares intimate conversations with the Almighty. He only writes what he hears. Keat hears or visually sees either the title or the first line. Nothing more comes until he starts to write. Then the words flow in poem form as a divine download, complete in one setting. Keat feels drawn into that supernatural realm until the words are complete. Then it lifts. The poems reflecting the Timing of God picture what God is doing in the supernatural realm, thus giving confirmation or direction.

Keat is a graduate of Fort Hays State University. He is a writer by desire and academically prepared with a Bachelor of Arts degree in English and Speech and a Master of Education degree in guidance and counseling. Keat retired from his teaching at Oklahoma Wesleyan University. Keat and Judy Garlow Wade now live in the San Diego area where his prophetic writing began.

Foreword

God is restoring our vision with provision.

Dr. Barbie Breathitt's *IMAGINE* series persuasively inspires Believers to embark on a journey of self-discovery, seeking and finding God and to discover His hidden, concealed mysteries through their sanctified imagination.

Readers will be immersed in God's truth and transformed by fresh revelation, soundly based on Scripture, crucial to this new season of operating in supernatural strength, powerful influence and Christ's authority. One is introduced to the aspects and mighty functions of the Holy Spirit, the Seven Spirits of God, God's communication conduits (dreams and visions) and how to use the awakened imagination to pray effectively, tap into unlimited favor and blessings, access healing and manifest miracles.

This is a new day of opportunity. Our divine imagination affords us the ability to know and receive all that God has destined for us to be and accomplish. It is time to increase and expand our borders. Barbie's writings challenge us to disconnect from the religious, legalistic ways of reasoning and exchange them for the creative, life-giving mind of Christ.

These volumes stir us to imagine the impossible, to consider how we think, what we believe and how we relate to God Almighty and others so that we can become Christlike, accurately discern God's plans and purposes and manifest His glory for His Kingdom advancement. Barbie has managed to successfully use applicable Scripture-based examples and captivating stories throughout the series to enlighten, encourage and guide us through a spiritual conversion of our identity that empowers us to apprehend our extraordinary future.

Our God-designed, ingenious imagination births visions of the unknown things of God and brings the invisible realms of creation into focus so it can become a reality in our lives. What we create and see in our imagination causes us to encounter and experience a broader dimension of God.

God's Spirit is advancing and positioning us through the use of our divine imagination to equip us with wisdom, revelation, fresh anointings and unlimited prosperity in order to draw the lost, sick and dying unto Christ.

Dr. John P. Kelly
Convener, International Coalition of Apostolic Leaders
InternationalCoalitionofApostolicLeaders.com

Contents

Endorsements vii
Works by the Author xi
Dedication xv
Thank You xvii
Foreword xix
Introduction 1
CHAPTER ONE True Vision vs True Blindness 7
CHAPTER TWO A Pure Heart with Divine Desire 13
CHAPTER THREE God's Universal Language of Love 27
CHAPTER FOUR Transformation into Transition 35
CHAPTER FIVE Spiritual Transition 47
CHAPTER SIX Keys to Success 53
CHAPTER SEVEN Free Will Choices 65
CHAPTER EIGHT For Such a Time as This 73
CHAPTER NINE Focused Faith 81
CHAPTER TEN Spiritual Intuition 89
CHAPTER ELEVEN Creative Power 95
CHAPTER TWELVE Connection—The Law of Attraction 103
CHAPTER THIRTEEN Fruitful Growth by Persevering 117
CHAPTER FOURTEEN Creative Transformation 125
CHAPTER FIFTEEN God's Answer for Healing 131
CHAPTER SIXTEEN The Imaginative Dreamer 139
CHAPTER SEVENTEEN Sons of God Arising 147

About the Author 157
Additional Resources 159

Introduction

As we come to a close on this *IMAGINE* journey together, this fifth volume of the series brings full circle all the previously learned concepts and revelations. With God's creative power, we can use godly disciplines of the imagination and divine desire to successfully maintain and faithfully steward our new, Christlike identity. As we prophesy as God commands and directs, we can successfully advance and prosper as Sons of God and as One New Man. With the propelling faith of God, we can believe, see and achieve our grandest, God-purposed destiny.

Our god-designed imagination creates our belief system. All Things that we believe and hold as true animates our world. By resetting our priorities to build ourselves up in our most holy faith, we ascend higher in our loving thoughts, actions, works and kind deeds. We take on the substance of the force of whatever conditions we are presently conscious of being in our life. If we continue to believe in and sustain our current condition, we will begin to feel it in our body, and we will become one with our current reality.

Ideas are always ready to manifest, but they require a protective guardian one who is dedicated to becoming their safe steward, and one who is willing to boldly display original concepts and champion cutting-edge, innovative, enterprises. Otherwise, our creative ideas will remain dormant, hidden and just incubating in the realm of the Spirit.

Don't be afraid, nervous or reluctant to be an outrageously imaginative dreamer. Remember, *All Things* have their being in God. *All Things* that are possible dwell within our limitless God! I think of *All Things* as a spiritual being who must be embraced because he contains *All Things* that we will experience in life. Within the essence of *All Things* is both the good and bad, the holy and the unholy, joy and sorrow, tragedy and triumph, victory and defeat, wealth and poverty, love and hate, light and darkness, health and sickness as well as healing and disease.

The all-knowing God is our producer, director and audience. He, not man utilizes all of the things that one encounters in life to create a well-rounded person. We are here on the earth to love and please God, not man. The dreams and visions that God strategically and beautifully fashions in our imagination lead and direct us through All Things into our advantageous callings. They reveal our life's excellent purposes and extensive destiny. *And we know that 'All Things'* (both the positive and negative that enter into our lives) *work together for good to those who love God, to those who are the called according to His purpose* (Romans 8:28).

When we gaze into the future, our faith empowers us to see our dreams as a fulfilled fact. Faith is the appropriation of the certain hope that we have for a good and prosperous future. Our wonderful imagination gives us previews of future attractions, if we will only believe we are what we see.

Believers have faith in God. But to manifest a greater degree of our God-given abilities, we must have the faith of God! This increased measure of the faith of God working in us has the power to change our current, personal identity. When we operate in the God kind of faith, we will discover that our new, Christ-centered identity also transforms our destiny.

By embracing the necessary process of change, we bring the present realization of our vision into our *now*. When these changes are incorporated into our imagination, and subsequently mixed into our waking life, we act differently and become a new creature in Christ, clothed in the power of His righteousness. Without encouraging, supporting and consistently sustaining this new image as true, our destiny will not come to pass. That to which we hold as true will become fact in our life. Imaginative prayer and meditation on God's Word ignite the vision of our higher self that is still hidden and waiting on us to believe and agree with it. Therefore, its image and personality can come forth and manifest.

> *God, who at various times in history and in various ways spoke in time past to the fathers by the prophets, has in these last*

> *days spoken to us by His Son Jesus, whom He has appointed heir of 'All Things.' For through Christ Jesus, God created the panorama of 'All Things', and all time in the worlds. Jesus the Son being the brightness of God's splendor and radiant glory and the exact express image of His person, and upholding His mirror image. He holds 'All Things' together in the universe and expands it by the mighty power of His spoken Word, when He had by Himself purged all of our sins, sat down at the right hand of the Majesty on high, having become so much better than the angels, as He has by inheritance obtained a more excellent name than they* (Hebrews 1:1–4).

The Word of God is living truth and spirit life. It has the power to save the lost, resurrect the dead, heal the broken and free the captive from mental and emotional prisons. The Word of God opens the eyes of the blind and impoverished to see how to prosper, advance and even create wealth. All transformational changes take place when we agree with the suggestions, inspiring influences and commands of *it is written!*

When we are able to maintain our focused attention (and focused faith) upon our God-given purposes, creative power is released to accomplish *All Things*. To gain a greater measure or vision of God's power working in us, we need to focus our attention on seeking first the Kingdom of God. When we seek God first, His wisdom and provision will always follow. Perseverance is an essential key to successfully obtaining and maintaining what we desire or imagine.

Believe and receive that the imaginative, creative Spirit of Christ dwells within your imagination. With the awakening of your imagination you will discover 'All Things' that are possible. You are fully able to understand the mysteries of God, realize and embody what you dream about, prophesy it into existence and manifest the prophetic words spoken, which will allow you to fully achieve your destiny!

God, the master weaver, has woven together every detail of our lives to fit into His perfect plan. This weaving brings All Things good into the lives of those who love Him so that they can fulfill His designed purposes on the earth. God has decreed the following over each one of us:

> You are My favored Son or Daughter, and with My favor I

have crowned you as a king or queen. Today I become your heavenly Father (see Psalm 2:7)! I have released and saturated you with the depths of My mighty power to work My layered purposes into everything you do (see Psalm 92:5). I promise that IAM the holy, splendorous One who speaks from My triumphant sanctuary to measure out the abundant portions of My people's inheritance. I will secure the land as I promised you, for they are all still Mine! Judah will continue to produce My kings and lawgivers of justice and righteousness, and Ephraim will produce dread champions, warriors who are great and mighty in the Lord. Moab will become My lowly servant, and Edom will also serve My purposes on the earth. IAM lifting up a shout over the land of Philistia (see Psalm 108:7–9). Know that IAM has chosen Jacob for My own special purpose, and Israel is My delightful treasure (see Psalm 135:4). All Things that I have made will praise Me to fulfill their purposes. All of My godly lovers will bow before Me in worship for All the Things I have done for them (see Psalm 145:10). Now set your eyes on the straight and narrow path I have set before you. Be fixed in your kingdom purposes. Do not let the things of life distract you from your high calling (see Proverbs 4:25). For IAM the Lord who works All Things together to accomplish My purposes. Even the wicked have to conform to accomplish My plans; they are set aside for the day of disaster (see Proverbs 16:4). Know that people may have many ideas concerning My plans for their lives, but only My designs for their purposes will succeed in the end (see Proverbs 19:21).

Let Us Pray

Dear heavenly Father, please call to my remembrance everything I have read in the previous four editions of the *IMAGINE* series. Empower me to align with what is written to activate Your living Word of Truth within my life. Grant me Your creative power so that I can develop godly disciplines of imagination and divine desires to successfully maintain and faithfully steward my Christlike identity. Teach me to prophesy as You command so that I will prosper as a Son of God and as One New Man.

Father, I believe You. Help my unbelief to be diminished and erased by Your everlasting Spirit of Truth. Please build my spirits up in my most holy faith so that my thoughts and ways ascend higher. Let my deeds be kind. Activate my creativity so that I can birth that which is dormant or hidden in the realm of the Spirit. Empower me to see Your plans for me in dreams and visions so that I have a hope to prosper in my future. Empower me to operate in the God kind of faith that brings my future realization of Your visions into my now. Please awaken my imagination so that I can understand the mysteries of God, realize what I dream and then prophesy it into existence. Help me achieve the full measure of my God-given destiny in You. Amen.

CHAPTER ONE

True Vision vs True Blindness

We were all born blind. We must all be born again in order to have our spiritual eyes opened to see the Kingdom of God and His righteousness. The book of John, chapter 9, gives an account of a man who was born blind, but he supernaturally received his sight from Jesus—the Savior, Prophet, Light of the World, Friend and Healer:

> *Now as Jesus passed by, He saw a man who was blind from birth. And His disciples asked Him, saying, "Rabbi, who sinned, this man or his parents, that he was born blind?" Jesus answered, "Neither this man nor his parents sinned, but that the works of God should be revealed in him. I must work the works of Him who sent Me while it is day; the night is coming when no one can work. As long as I am in the world, I am the light of the world." When He had said these things, He spat on the ground and made clay with the saliva; and He anointed the eyes of the blind man with the clay. And He said to him, "Go, wash in the pool of Siloam (means sent)." So, he went and washed, and came back seeing.*
>
> *Therefore, the neighbors and those who previously had seen that he was blind said, "Is not this he who sat and begged?" Some said, "This is he." Others said, "He is like him." He said, "I AM he." Therefore, they said to him, "How were your eyes*

opened?" He answered and said, "A Man called Jesus made clay and anointed my eyes and said to me, 'Go to the pool of Siloam and wash.' So, I went and washed, and I received sight." Then they said to him, "Where is He?" He said, "I do not know."

There are those who will choose to remain blind, those who remain wedged in the religious or carnal mindset. There may be times when we have to fly solo as we advance in the Kingdom of God. We must continue when others choose to remain blind and in a religious mindset. We must always resist shrinking back into what the world commands as truth, even when others direct us otherwise.

They brought him who formerly was blind to the Pharisees. Now it was a Sabbath when Jesus made the clay and opened his eyes. Then the Pharisees also asked him again how he had received his sight. He said to them, "He put clay on my eyes, and I washed, and I see." Therefore, some of the Pharisees said, "This Man is not from God, because He does not keep the Sabbath." Others said, "How can a man who is a sinner do such signs?" And there was a division among them. They said to the blind man again, "What do you say about Him because He opened your eyes?" He said, "He is a prophet."

But the Jews did not believe concerning him, that he had been blind and received his sight, until they called the parents of him who had received his sight. And they asked them, saying, "Is this your son, who you say was born blind? How then does he now see?" His parents answered them and said, "We know that this is our son, and that he was born blind; but by what means he now sees we do not know, or who opened his eyes we do not know. He is of age; ask him. He will speak for himself." His parents said these things because they feared the Jews, for the Jews had agreed already that if anyone confessed that He was Christ, he would be put out of the synagogue. Therefore, his parents said, "He is of age; ask him."

So, they again called the man who was blind, and said to him, "Give God the glory! We know that this Man is a sinner." He answered and said, "Whether He is a sinner or not I do not know. One thing I know: that though I was blind, now I see."

Then they said to him again, "What did He do to you? How did He open your eyes?" He answered them, "I told you already, and you did not listen. Why do you want to hear it again? Do you also want to become His disciples?" Then they reviled him and said, "You are His disciple, but we are Moses' disciples. We know that God spoke to Moses; as for this fellow, we do not know where He is from." The man answered and said to them, "Why, this is a marvelous thing, that you do not know where He is from; yet He has opened my eyes! Now we know that God does not hear sinners; but if anyone is a worshiper of God and does His will, He hears him. Since the world began it has been unheard of that anyone opened the eyes of one who was born blind. If this Man were not from God, He could do nothing." They answered and said to him, "You were completely born in sins, and are you teaching us?" And they cast him out.

Jesus heard that they had cast him out; and when He had found him, He said to him, "Do you believe in the Son of God?" He answered and said, "Who is He, Lord, that I may believe in Him?" And Jesus said to him, "You have both seen Him and it is He who is talking with you."

The blind man had never seen Jesus before. He had only heard Jesus instructing him, "Go wash." The man was still blind when Jesus, the master potter, spat on the ground to form clay eyes out of the dust of the earth. Jesus' spit contained His healing blood and water. The healing life of Jesus' DNA was mingled in the clay eyes (mask) that touched the blind man's eyes. Jesus sent him to the pool of Siloam to wash.

Then he said, "Lord, I believe!" And he worshiped Him. And Jesus said, "For judgment I have come into this world, that those who do not see may see, and that those who see may be made blind." Then some of the Pharisees who were with Him heard these words, and said to Him, "Are we blind also?" Jesus said to them, "If you were blind, you would have no sin; but now you say, 'We see.' Therefore, your sin remains."

When we are born again, our carnal blindness is replaced with the divine light of spiritual sight. Through our Christ-conscious, divine imagination, we are able to see clearly in the Spirit. If we can see what is happening in the invisible Spirit realm, we can do the impossible by cooperating with the power of Christ within. *Therefore, we do not lose heart. Even though our outward* (physical body) *man is perishing, yet the inward* (imaginative spirit) *man is being renewed day by day* (2 Corinthians 4:16).

Saul's transformation is a perfect example. On the road to Damascus, Saul saw the brilliant light of God's Merkava chariot. He fell to the ground blinded. The Spirit led Saul into and through a visionary and transformational wilderness that took years in order for him to become the Apostle Paul. The kingdom gospel Paul taught was shown to him by the Holy Spirit. The scales were removed from Paul's eyes, so he could see truth and revelation knowledge by heaven's bright light. This is why the Apostle Paul did not continue to carry on the religious traditions of man (see Acts 18; 19). Paul was pregnant with divine destiny, a holy purpose and creative spiritual concepts. Paul was awakened to the vision realm and was retrained by the Holy Spirit for three years. During that time, the Holy Spirit was birthing a church in Ephesus in order to give us a spiritual inheritance.

> *We must always resist shrinking back into what the world commands as truth, even when others direct us otherwise.*

Let Us Pray

Dear Jesus, Your Word states that without a revelatory vision from You that points ahead to an appointed end time, people run wild like lost sheep without a shepherd to guide them. Please open my eyes to see what You and the Father are doing, because if I cannot see what You are doing in my prayers and dreams, I will trip, stumble and fall all over myself. I know genuine happiness and the joy of Your strength rest in me because I adhere to Your instructions. Thank You for empowering me to attend to what You have revealed so that IAM most blessed.

I know that Your Word cannot lie; it will accomplish that which You have sent it to do. Even if there is a delay, I will wait for it;

for I know that it is coming into fullness in my life. Help me to bathe in Your Word so that the scales are washed from my eyes. I want to see the light of Your beautiful face. As I gaze upon Your grandeur, impregnate my womb with Your plans so I can birth everything You desire for me as part of Your spiritual inheritance. Amen

CHAPTER TWO

A Pure Heart with Divine Desire

The Bible states that the pure in heart will see God. When we seek God with all of our heart, He will be found by us. To change our circumstances and the state of our existence, we must become a new living being. To bring about these changes, we must choose creative visions and positive, productive words to speak within our heart's imagination. We have learned that the subconscious imagination always sees, hears and announces the same vision that has been impressed upon it by our conscious mind (please refer to Volumes I and IV for a detailed refresher). When we start listening to the voice of the Holy Spirit, we will hear and say what God says. We will see and do what God does. *Blessed are the pure in heart; for they shall see God* (Matthew 5:8).

Our God is the giver of All Things. He continually looks for opportunities to bless us. Many people find it difficult to trust God, even when He wants to give them good things. They have not developed an ability to hear or recognize the voice of God speaking into their life, so they do not respond to His gentle nudges. People hear the Word but don't really take it to heart or implement the changes. Others hear the truth in their head but do not apply it in their hearts, so it is never lived out in their life.

> We are to be not only hearers of the Word but also doers of the Word, otherwise we only deceive ourselves. Do not fool yourself. For if anyone is just a hearer of the Word, thinking that is what matters most, and is not a doer of what

God requires, by putting things into action, he is like a man observing his natural face in a mirror. One minute he looks at himself, goes away, and immediately forgets what he looks like and what kind of person he was. However, it is possible to open your eyes and take in the beautiful, perfect truth of God's Word found in God's law of liberty and live by it. If you pursue that higher path and actually do what God has commanded, then you will be blessed and avoid the many distractions that lead to an amnesia of All true Things. If you think of yourself more highly than you ought, by talking a good game and considering yourself to be the ultimate role model in All Things religious, but you cannot control your tongue, then think again. You have been deceived because your mouth exposes the inner working of your heart, and your religion is proven to be worthless. Real religion is kind, generous and full of love. It reaches out to the orphan and the widow, the homeless and loveless in their plight, and it guards against corruption and injustice in a godless world (see James 1:22–26).

If we take on the image and likeness of the Christ who dwells within us, we will manifest that same likeness to the world. After we have transformed into the image of Christ, the people we knew before our transformation will notice the positive changes in us when they meet us again, and they will want to know God too! Having a pure heart means that we have a clean, clear Christ consciousness.

Every creative idea or positive image of our new identity begins within the Spirit of Christ that is dwelling within our imagination. A positive, fruitful imagination will increase the dimensional scope and authority of our influence.

Personal Reflection Moment

1. How do you view yourself?
2. What types of influences do you allow in your life?
3. Are you the master creator of your world or an indentured slave to all? Will you become the builder, owner, investor or just remain the renter?

4. Are you jealous or resentful of others?

5. What type of attitudes do you manifest? Are you hopeful, positive and expectant of being favored with good success? Or do you expect the worst, living a life of fear or full of dread?

In order to prosper, we must develop a positive thought life that is always optimistic. We need to unite our affirmative thoughts with our upbeat, inner conversational voice that speaks with a definite expectancy of a specific successful and confident future end. By constructing an encouraging vision of our end result, our future actions will be certain to acquire and fulfill our desires of prosperity. *And if we know that He hears us in whatever we ask, we also know that we have obtained the requests we ask of Him* (1 John 5:15).

The perfect, absolute peace of God's presence surrounds those whose imaginations are consumed with confidently trusting Him (see Isaiah 26:3). This is true because their imagination can see beyond any perceived limitations into the broad expanses of All Things possible. God's divine light will illuminate the eyes of our imaginations, flooding us with illuminating radiance, until we experience the full revelation of the hope of His calling, which is the wealth of God's glorious inheritance that He find in us, His holy people (see Ephesians 1:18)!

> *Every creative idea or positive image of our new identity begins within the Spirit of Christ that is dwelling within our imagination.*

We are never to doubt God's mighty power that works in us to accomplish All Things. Christ has the ability to accomplish infinitely more that our greatest request our most unbelievable dream. He has the immeasurable power to exceed our wildest imagination! God will outdo them all, for His miracle, Dunamis, resurrection power is constantly energizing us (see Ephesians 3:20).

The Hebrew word for imagination in these passages is yester. This creative word means *the power of the imaginative mind to form a concept that will build a new framework or structure*. The perfect peace of God inspires the imagination to build a foundation of trust so He can pour out His revelation power on a holy people who have been created in His image.

The creative Word of God is living, quick and powerful. When our imagination is trained to prophesy and draw on the Word of God, our thoughts, conversations and actions will develop an unshakable faith. The (Word of God) seeds that we think on, decree and plant in our life will create fruit after their kind.

Our inner speech always mirrors our mental state of being. Our imagination is continually attracting to itself what we are currently. Believers cannot separate themselves from the Christ that is within their imagination. While our positive words create a prosperous life, our negative words call forth disease, death, despair and depression that form dark, destructive actions within our being. Positive inner speech creates the radiant light of life and prosperity. It opens many doors of opportunity.

The wise person will always create more opportunity than is offered. The proceeding Word of God manifests the positive energy that is needed to generate what we want by producing the person who we desire to be. Success comes from discovering opportunities in difficulties. If opportunity does not come knocking, learn how to construct a double door.

Hidden opportunities are usually masquerading as hard work, so most people don't acknowledge them. If someone propositions you with a remarkable opportunity, but you are not certain you can do it, agree to and accept the prospect, then ascertain how to do it later. Determine what you want, then decide and act like it is impossible to fail.

> The creative Word of God is living, quick and powerful.

If we replay the same negative words over and over in our mind, they will detract from our vital energy, which leads to our defeat. Morbid words form an environment of poverty; they construct lack and disease. *Therefore, lay aside all filthiness and overflow of wickedness, and receive with meekness the implanted Word, which is able to save your souls* (James 1:21).

Jesus taught His disciples to go in His authority and make disciples of all nations, baptizing them in the name of the Father, the Son and the Holy Spirit. We are to teach people how to observe all that Jesus commanded. Jesus encouraged us, *Behold IAM always with you every day, even until the end of the age* (Matthew 28:20). We are spirits that have been gifted with the power to gain access to the mind of Christ, and we are spirits with the ability to speak His Word with a creative authority.

To please God, Believers must subdue the old nature by changing their former conversations. When we revolutionize the way we think, speak and act, we are able to put on a new, godly image. We exchange an old, tattered, rough coat for a seamless, smooth, pure silk garment of righteousness. A more excellent spiritual mantle gives us entrance into another state of Christ consciousness. Our new nature aligns with God's. His presence within our life causes us to be in right standing with God. When we are righteous, we can live a powerful life in an upright manner.

> *When we revolutionize the way we think, speak and act, we are able to put on a new, godly image.*

Believers have put on a new, regenerated nature that has been recreated in God's image in His true righteousness and holiness. We have been born again into regeneration, not from a mortal origin of the seed and sperm but from an immortal (spiritual) seed that recreates us by the eternal, everlasting Word of God.

When we have a longing desire to exhibit a higher state of being (one of grace, love or full of gratitude), we please God. By taking on a higher state of being, God is able to pour out more spiritual insights, enlightening us to His eternal love, unlimited power, wisdom and revelation knowledge. His higher ways are unfolded to us as we are given more understanding of His great salvation (see Psalm 50:23).

> *And He has taught you to let go of the lifestyle of the ancient man, the old self-life, which was carnal, corrupted by sinful and deceitful desires that spring from delusions. Now it's time to be made new by every revelation that's been given to you. And to be transformed as you embrace the glorious Christ-within as your new life. We live in union with Him! For God has re-created you all over again in His perfect righteousness, and you now belong to Him in the realm of true holiness* (Ephesians 4:22–24).

Personal Reflection Moment

1. Do you consider yourself pure of heart?
2. Are you a negative, critical or judgmental person, always assuming the worst?
3. Do you dislike yourself? Do you expect others to reject you?

May I suggest that you repent from answers that do not align with God's truth? From now on, open yourself up to only positive, godly influences.

Learn how to break destructive, bad habits. Begin to invest your time in the Bible. Invest your money in resources that will feed your spirit to produce positive beliefs, beautiful images and life-giving thoughts in order to prosper. God wants to cause you to increase! *I sent you to reap that for which you have not labored; others have labored, and you have entered into their labors* (John 4:38).

Discipline your thought life to think exclusively on Christlike things that are of a true reality. Think on things that are magnificent, impartial and unprejudiced, whatever things are pure and lovely, whatever things are of a good report. If there is any virtue and anything praiseworthy—meditate, *'meletao'* imagine, on these things (see Philippians 4:8).

Practice using the wisdom found in the above referenced positive, creative and powerful verse to change the way you think about and act toward the difficult people in your life. Make an effort to find at least one great thing they are good at, then celebrate them for that one thing. Search for one more good attribute until you can find two positive things to admire.

> *By taking on a higher state of being, God is able to pour out more spiritual insights, enlightening us to His eternal love, unlimited power, wisdom and revelation knowledge.*

Pretty soon your negative perspective will change into a lovely, expectant and praiseworthy good report.

Know exactly what you desire in life. Do not sell yourself short or compromise your God-given desires in anyway. Nothing is impossible with God. Faithfully speak life-giving words that are fruitful, words that build up and edify yourself and others. Focus on a positive state of being, even if it means denying what your natural senses are currently telling you. The imagination is only limited by your level of determined and forward motivation to believe and have faith to see how to create and obtain your future.

Doing this will draw that higher future state of prosperity into your now circumstances. Let yourself feel and experience what it would be like to have already obtained that desire. Begin to explore success. Let those feelings of joy into your imagination. Continue to envision them until they become a now reality to you.

The inner conversations that we carry on with ourselves are not only heard by us but are also mentally recorded by us. They are also quiet personal prayers and petitions that are heard by God. What have you been creating and asking for?

The type of silent words that we continually rehearse and decree over and over again will either encourage prosperity in the future or form threatening weapons. The thoughts we meditate upon and the words we speak create the action we take. Words set the courses of our life. Words are the wellspring sources of either life or death, so always carefully choose your words with great wisdom.

When we are able to align the thoughts of our mind with the spirit of our heart, our conversation will come into agreement with the higher thoughts and fuse with the better ways of God.

When we are able to align the thoughts of our mind with the spirit of our heart, our conversation will come into agreement with the higher thoughts and fuse with the better ways of God. *Again, I say to you that if two of you agree* (two separate people agreeing or both the subconscious and conscious or spirit and soul within one person aligning with God's truth) *on earth concerning anything that they ask, it will be done for them by My Father in heaven* (Matthew 18:19).

If our conscious desires agree with our subconscious desires there is a strong alliance of unified belief that is formed. This oneness of thought, coalition of purpose and faith-filled, cooperative actions, releases the commanded blessing of our heavenly Father. *Behold, how good and how pleasant it is for brethren to dwell together in unity! For there the Lord commanded the blessing—Life forevermore* (Psalm 133:1–3).

The people we interact with on a daily basis will conform to the image and perception that we hold of them. We unknowingly project (subconsciously) all of our inner thoughts about them to them. The silent conversations we hold within as being true about people also have the power to form an entrance door of favor or an exit door of disfavor.

Because people will always respond in some way or manner to the subconscious messages that we send to them, we are to demonstrate love by loving our neighbor as much as we love ourself. Jesus taught us to love the Lord our God with every passion of our heart, with all the energy of our being, with every thought and with all the strength that is within us. Love is the greatest commandment of all. Love completes the laws of God. Jesus also instructed us to love our enemies (see Matthew 5:43). We will never find a more important commandment than these (see Galatians 5:14; Luke 10:27; Mark 12:33; Matthew 22:36–40). Love is the creative force contained within the sanctified imagination.

> *Faith comes by hearing, believing and empowering our imagination to act upon the Word of God.*

Although the Godhead is three distinct persons, they all love, counsel with, submit to and prefer each other. The three-in-one Godhead agree with each other and always function as a unified force of One. *That they all may be one, as You, Father, are in Me, and I in You; that they also may be one in Us, that the world may believe that You sent Me* (John 17:21).

When we are pure in heart, we will stop suffering. We will be spiritually enlightened, and the desires of our imagination will be in harmony with God's perfect will. Our thoughts form the mental and spoken words that create our environment and world. Therefore, the words we speak govern every aspect of our life. We are what we think, speak, hear, see, dream, receive, believe and act upon. We emerge as the person we were created to become when we refuse to murmur and complain. Instead of being negative, we continually pray for and execute justice and righteousness in order to rule and reign in a spirit of excellence.

Righteousness

A person of dignity will stand up and fight for what is right, just and good, especially if it is for the rights of the innocent unborn. *Righteousness and justice are the foundation of Your throne; mercy and truth go before Your face* (Psalm 89:14).

God's law and commandments are the divine principles of the universe. *He made you king over them, to do justice and righteousness* (2 Chronicles 9:8).

God's justice is the substance upon which All Things are built and settled. *He loves righteousness and justice; the earth is full of the goodness of the Lord* (Psalm 33:5).

God's righteousness frames and shapes the structure of our spiritual government and the very fibers of our being. *He shall bring forth your righteousness as the light, and your justice as the noonday* (Psalm 37:6).

When we walk with God, He clothes us in the light of His righteousness, power and presence. *I put on righteousness, and it clothed me; my justice was like a robe and a turban* (Job 29:14).

For a person to judge God's world in righteousness, they must first discover and establish their own uprightness. We increase in godliness by sustaining our morality; we continually develop more virtue and decency. *He will judge Your people with righteousness, and Your poor with justice* (Psalm 72:2).

When people repent and change their thoughts to reflect God's honesty, others will repent and will be drawn to the morally good light of their integrity shining. When we search our heart, repent for our wrong thoughts and transform the way we think and imagine, the world around us will change for the good. Inner thoughts cannot

To experience positive change, we must move our faith into the now, present moment and assume a different state of being or higher belief.

be retained inside our being as a secret that only we contemplate or rehearse. Once a thought is birthed, it grows and forms an action that becomes a habitual pattern that forces change.

Faith comes by hearing, believing and empowering our imagination to act upon the Word of God.

> *If you remain in Me and My Words remain in you, ask whatever you wish, and it will be done for you. This is to My Father's glory, that you bear much fruit, showing yourselves to be My disciples* (John 15:7–8).

After our soul hears the Word or dreams a dream, we must allow a positive image to form. Therefore, we can actively yield in obedience to formulate and shape a correct response. Instead of believing you are sick, poor, inadequate, alone or weak, say the truth of what God says about you and your situation: "IAM healed in Christ. IAM rich in Christ. IAM adequate in Christ. IAM strong in the power of His might!"

The opinion you hold about yourself will determine the measure of success you experience in life. Repent of all sin, negative confessions, fear, doubt and unbelief. Living out of our bright imagination, not our dark fears, will create an amazing, new world of beauty and fulfilled opportunities. Ask for a new vision to move you into a greater measure of faith. Stop postponing the arrival of your answers to prayer with statements that begin with *I will be* instead of *IAM*. The profession of *I will be* indicates that you are currently *not*. It indicates that you do not currently have the faith to believe that you *are*; therefore, you *are not*.

To experience positive change, we must move our faith into the now, present moment and assume a different state of being or higher belief. Then we must maintain that new image, thought or identity. Your new identity is waiting to be embodied by you. We are to pray always believing and not faint.

> *Why would you ever complain, saying, "God has lost track of me. He doesn't care what happens to me?" Don't you know anything? Haven't you been listening? God doesn't come and go. God lasts. He's Creator of all you can see or imagine. He doesn't get tired out, doesn't pause to catch His breath. And*

> *He knows everything, inside and out. God gives power to the weak, and to those who have no might He increases strength. He energizes those who get tired, gives fresh strength to drop-outs. For even young people get tire, weary, faint and drop out, young folk in their prime stumble and fall. But those who wait upon God get fresh strength. They spread their wings, catch a new wind of the Spirit and soar like eagles, they run and are not weary or get tired, they walk and don't lag behind or faint* (Isaiah 40:29–31).

Stop blaming outside circumstances and others for your current state of being. The Christ in you has the answers that you need. Look to your inner mountain range, ascend to the north, and seek the face of God. For it is from your internal hills that God, your hope, will spring. *I will lift up my eyes to the hills—from whence comes my help? My help comes from the Lord, Who made heaven and earth* (Psalm 121:1–2).

Take personal responsibility, and repent for your own doubt-filled actions, for the wrong things you have thought, said and believed. When you stand praying, claim, confess and believe that you are who you desire to be. Consciously assume the part of God's divine nature that you need for your very own new nature.

God's divine nature will manifest in the people who have repented, have cleaned their hands from wrong and have a godly, righteous imagination (a pure, faith-filled heart). Grace and peace will be multiplied to us in and through the knowledge of God and His ways.

> *God's divine power has granted to us everything pertaining to life and godliness, through the true knowledge of Him Who called us by His own glory and excellence. For by these He has granted to us His precious and magnificent promises, so that by them you may become partakers of the divine nature, having escaped the corruption that is in the world by lust* (2 Peter 1:3–5).

Prayer, dreams and visions empower us to see the invisible realms of the Spirit.

> *For since the creation of the world God's invisible attributes,*

> *His eternal power and divine nature, have been clearly seen, being understood through what has been made, so that they are without excuse. For even though they knew God, they did not honor Him as God or give thanks, but they became futile in their speculations, and they're foolish heart was darkened. Professing to be wise, they became fools, and exchanged the glory of the incorruptible God for an image in the form of corruptible man and of birds and four-footed animals and crawling creatures* (Romans 1:20–23).

To obtain the divine nature, we must diligently apply our faith to provide moral excellence in the knowledge of God, to exercise self-control, perseverance and godliness. These all lead to brotherly kindness and love (see 2 Peter 1:5–8). Kingdom gifts, blessings and anointings will increase our prosperity according to the measure of faith and spiritual understanding we possess. The amount of the knowledge of God, His ways and wisdom that we possess will empower us to obtain houses we did not build and harvest lands we did not buy or plant.

Jesus is always desirous of giving us a new mansion that is built in heavenly places as a reward for seeking after Him with all of our heart. The level of power and authority we possess, manifest and exercise, in the realms of both the natural world and in the spiritual influences, are determined by the degree that our new man has been renewed by the Word of God. We must be transformed by the Spirit, and then we must be conformed to the image of Christ Jesus' divine, holy nature. The presence of Christ in us empowers us to obtain God's glory so that we can arise and shine forth with His presence.

Let Us Pray

Dear Jesus, cleanse me from all sin, and purify the conscious of my heart so that I can see You in all of Your radiant beauty. Fill my heart with Your creative words, and make me into a new creature in Christ. God, I know that You hear me when I pray, so open my ears to hear what the Trinity is saying to each other. Remove the scales from my eyes so that I can see what is going on in heaven. Place a guard upon my mouth so that it only speaks positive, life-giving words. Give me the wisdom and necessary skills to bring Your Kingdom out of me so that I can display Your majesty on earth. Help me to view myself the way You see me—as a new, regenerated creature in Christ. Let my mind dwell in a higher place to think Your superior thoughts.

Thank you for giving me full access to Your mind, to speak forth Your will with authority. I repent of my sins, so You can manifest Your divine nature through me. Please establish me in Your righteousness so that I can continue to develop more virtue, moral excellence and decency and walk covered in Your glory. Amen.

CHAPTER THREE

God's Universal Language of Love

At the Tower of Babel, man had one language. God determined that mankind had unified itself with one goal of reaching the heavens through the building of a star tower. Nimrod unified man under socialism and the banner of secular humanism, demanding that people commune with and worship other gods. Looking upon the self-destructive evil found in man's heart, God, in His mercy, confused man's language. A great earthquake separated the one land mass into seven different continents, which disbursed man to the four corners of the earth. God knew that if man had one language, nothing would be impossible for them to accomplish.

Today, there is only one universal language that exists on earth today. That one language, common to all people, is God's spiritual, symbolic love language of dreams. God-given dreams inspire man to accomplish amazing feats that would be impossible without God's wisdom and strategy. Dreams bring impossibilities into the realm of possibilities.

Before the foundation of the world, God fashioned vision and placed dreams within the heart of every person. These God-given dreams are love letters that are designed to draw us back to God. Dreams and visions empower us to discover that God is our Source and Creator. These God-inspired dreams appear at the perfect time. Their interpretations prophesy to us the scope of our gifts and passionate mission in life.

Dreams and visions lead and direct us into our callings, and they announce our life's purposes and grand destiny. *And the Lord said, "Indeed the people are one and they all have one language, and this is what they begin to do; now nothing that they propose to do will be withheld from them"* (Genesis 11:6).

If Believers in Christ would unite as one people, God could direct us to worldwide success through the dreams He has placed within each of us. The power of a unified team of Believers, the awakened Ecclesia of God, is an unstoppable force. When Believers unite in love and in God's kingdom purposes, while moving in the power of the Holy Spirit, nothing will be impossible.

> Dreams and visions lead and direct us into our callings, and they announce our life's purposes and grand destiny.

Positive change comes when we repent of keeping our old nature alive. When we surrender all of our negative self-images to Christ, they are forgiven and removed. God replaces our old, sinful nature with His new ideas, positive attributes, higher powers and progressive, proceeding and life-giving words.

Agreeing with God's divine plans for your life quickly moves you from one level of thought into a higher dimension of God's presence and thought. When you agree with God, you are given spiritual sight to see your reflection mirroring Christ. The manifest presence of Christ causes you to feel and experience the changes that have taken place in you, knowing that you have become your new, desired reality. *So shall My Word be that goes forth from My mouth; it shall not return to Me void, but it shall accomplish what I please, and it shall prosper in the thing for which I sent it* (Isaiah 55:11).

Now is the acceptable time for salvation. As we continue to picture our new identity, focusing on our new image, we are being transformed by the glory of God that creates a new, tender heart of flesh within us. *Of His own will He brought us forth by the Word of truth, that we might be a kind of firstfruits of His creatures* (James 1:18).

God has placed the power of His Word near us for our continual access. His Word is in our mouth, so we can always speak forth life. The internal words that we speak frame and create the outer world that manifests around us.

When we hear the still, small voice of Christ resounding within us, we will also hear it loudly proclaimed by us into our outer world. God's Word is written upon the tablets of our hearts so that we can choose to believe and decree God's Word from the roof and mountain tops. The Word of God creates a good life, so we have the power and dominion to overcome sin, lack, death and evil.

We walk in the powerful ways of God when we choose to live a blessed, abundant life. Our inner conversations must agree with Christ's speech in order to cause the words we think to enter into and take root in our emotional arena. Our emotions have a lasting effect on us. The weight of our emotions produces the speech that frames our desires. Our emotions inspire us to take physical actions in order to gain our aims in life.

The Spirit of the Lord shares the concepts of God with us. It is the good pleasure of Jesus Christ to adopt us as His Sons. The creative words that are on our tongue empower us to be imitators of God. When we copy God's ways, we ascend into a higher revelatory plain of existence. One of our aims in life must be to know God as Creator. We must pant after knowing and drinking in Christ, just as the thirsty deer pants after the water brook (see Psalm 42:1).

If we refuse to embrace the image of a higher concept of ourself, we will continue to remain the same, unchanged, common and ordinary person who is always struggling to obtain the promise of a better future. However, if we desire God with all our heart and submit to His plans of prosperity and success, when Jesus visits us in dreams, visions and prayerful meditations, He will receive and transform us unto Himself. A divine exchange takes place, so where He is dwelling in a higher state of liberty, we can go to be with Him there also.

The internal words that we speak frame and create the outer world that manifests around us.

Christ sets our imagination free by reforming the old image that we have held of ourself. Christ performs His will, words and good pleasure toward us by causing us to be transformed into His likeness. When we return to a prosperous place in God, we are able to dwell in a new mansion or state of consciousness as a new being that has taken on and now reflects God's image.

> *For I know the thoughts that I think toward you, says the LORD, thoughts of peace and not of evil, to give you a future and a hope. Then you will call upon Me and go and pray to Me, and I will listen to you. And you will seek Me and find Me, when you search for Me with all your heart. I will be found by you, says the LORD, and I will bring you back from your captivity; I will gather you from all the nations and from all the places where I have driven you, says the LORD, and I will bring you to the place from which I cause you to be carried away captive* (Jeremiah 29:11–13).

The natural mind cannot receive or understand the things of the Spirit, so we must develop the mind of Christ within our renewed spirit. *If you can? All Things are possible to him who believes* (Mark 9:23). This verse confirms that our part is to believe God. If we can believe God, All Things become possible. In Christ, our faith always begins with the end result in mind. Every time God speaks, the power of His words instantly creates the manifestation of His desire.

As joint heirs in Christ, we are created in God's image and likeness. Knowing that words create, we should proclaim, "I can do All Things through Christ Jesus who strengthens me." Never, ever state, "I can't!" about any situation in life. If these harmful words are spoken to the subconscious, it forms a false belief statement that generates a destructive lie, which takes up residence as one's personal internal truth.

When *I can't* manifests, it establishes doubt. *I cannot* creates a false truth in the subconscious. If this lie is believed and acted upon, it will build a mental stronghold that will, in turn, levy a self-imposed curse of limitation that will cause failure to manifest. By placing our faith in Christ Jesus, we believe in things that cannot be seen with the natural eyes. By faith, we connect our inner man of the spirit with the Holy Spirit. The work of the Holy Spirit causes us to gain access to the invisible realm.

> *When we return to a prosperous place in God, we are able to dwell in a new mansion or state of consciousness as a new being that has taken on and now reflects God's image.*

When we speak the Word of God to the concealed future, we open the passageway to bring the already formed, but not yet revealed, future into the now. Faith connects us to the future that was created at the earth's genesis so that it can be believed, seen, birthed and manifested into the immediate as a now reality. Believers have spirit eyes that can see the invisible realms of glory, angels, spirit beings, creatures, hosts, seraphim and cherubim. My best-selling book *Angels in God's Kingdom* goes into detail on how to discover and activate and minister and cooperate with and in these realms of glory.

Mary Magdalene saw into the realms of angels at Jesus' resurrection. But Mary's eyes were not able to visibly recognize Jesus when He stood before her in His manifested, higher resurrected form. However, Mary's ears were still tuned to His higher frequency, so she recognized Jesus' voice when He lovingly spoke her name, "Mary!"

The women who loved, served and followed Jesus were the initial ones to see Jesus first after His resurrection (see John 20; Matthew 16), while Jesus' close male friends were cowering. Even His disciples remained hidden behind closed doors. Jesus' disciples could not hear or enter in to seek Jesus; they were bound by their fear and personal traumas (see Luke 24). Believers have spiritual ears that can tune into the inaudible, still, small voice of the Holy Spirit. They can hear the resounding audible voice of God that lovingly beckons to them, "Come up here, and follow Me!"

> When we speak the Word of God to the concealed future, we open the passageway to bring the already formed, but not yet revealed, future into the now.

We can sense God's moods, the different manifestations of the moving of God's majestic hands, His all-seeing eyes and the stirring of the winds, when He moves His body or takes in a powerful breath. Believers feel the vibrations of God's presence, the heat and burning fire of His presence, His gentle kisses and warm loving embrace. Believers know God's mercy, grace and extreme passion toward His Bride.

The Holy Spirit's movements have intensified. The Spirit comes to break the power of every evil occult cycle in our lives. He easily destroys the strongholds that these lies have formed in our mind. Christians are living in the best of times for the Kingdom of Light. Yet it is the worst of times for the sinful kingdom of darkness! God has rent the heavens to come down to judge lying, deceptive spirits (see Isaiah 64:1). The Spirit of God does terrible, mighty, unexpected things that will shake up the mountains of liberal resistance. The Spirit of God brings their rebellious acts down in order to rock their foundations, so that they can repent and be saved.

The fire of the Holy Spirit has come to burn up the wood, hay and stubble of His adversaries. Nations will tremble and quake at God's presence. God is showing Himself strong and active on behalf of the Believers who have been prayerfully waiting in His presence. With God's direction, strategy and help, we can achieve anything we put our minds to. Remember, greatness always involves brokenness, change and a transitional transformation. Brokenness is a process that when one is fully healed, his or her restoration leads to a new strength. Healing means that we have chosen to live and to get better without any regrets.

> With God's direction, strategy and help, we can achieve anything we put our minds to.

Personal Reflection Moment

1. What do you believe? What type of person are you? What type of person do you want to be?
2. What type of person has Christ called you to become?
3. How are you known in heaven? How are you known on earth? How do you want to be known in heaven and on earth?
4. Have you tapped into the glory and all of the divine resources that are available to you?

There are no limitations or small boundaries in God. He will never limit or box us in. Go ahead, take a leap of faith! Remember that we always get our wings on the way down. God is calling us to stand up and boldly represent His Kingdom wherever we have been planted.

Let Us Pray

Dear Lord Jesus, ignite the dreams that You have hidden within me. Give me skill and understanding of Your symbolic love letters. Make me one with You in spirit and in truth. Show me Your divine purposes for my life so that I can agree to accomplish Your perfect will for me. Thank you for adopting me as a Son of God, as a joint heir to Christ. I choose to take on a higher image of myself that will reflect Your grace, mercy and power here on earth. Help me to access and develop the mind of Christ.

I repent of all doubt, unbelief and failure that have touched my subconscious. Open my eyes, like You opened Mary's, to see You in Your transcendent and spiritual forms. Burn up all of the wood, hay and stubble that I have collected in my life. Increase my boundaries as You did for Jabez, removing all pain, sorrow and disappointments of the past. Amen.

CHAPTER FOUR

Transformation into Transition

God reveals Himself to us at the level of our spiritual hunger and desire. The Priest Eli had stopped seeking God with his whole heart, and he neglected to discipline his sons, so his eyes were darkened and nearly blind. The loss of his passion had caused the lamp of God's revelatory light to diminish to the point that the candle had almost gone out.

The Word of the Lord was rare, and the visions of God were infrequent. A nation of people was perishing. There is always a death of the old in a transitional season so that the new wineskin can be formed. Prophet Seer Samuel, who was taught by Eli, both saw and heard the Lord's coming. This spiritual increase brought forth and established a new era of hearing, seeing and prophesying words that did not fall to the ground.

We find ourselves in the very same new era today. The seer anointing that opened our eyes to be able see into the invisible realms of the Spirit was poured out for the last ten years. Now the era of the mouth has begun. The time of the open prophetic mouth has come for the anointed Believers, pastors, evangelists, teachers, prophets and apostolic voices to rise to a place of international influence as they decree, declare and prophesy the Word of the Lord with signs and creative wonders following.

Isn't it interesting that at the end of 2019 and the start of the 2020 era, a (man-made) worldwide Coronavirus outbreak spread into a pandemic? Or should I call it what it is—a planned-demic? The virus is called the Wuhan virus (commonly referred to as COVID-19) because it was manufactured in a laboratory that originated in the small Chinese village of Wuhan. China quarantined the whole city of Wuhan and prevented anyone from entering any part of China. However, the infected people in China were allowed and encouraged to board planes to visit any worldwide destination.

Now that the virus has systematically spread throughout the cities of the world, everyone's mouths are being covered by masks to supposedly prevent the further spread of this respiratory virus. In reality, the wearing of masks only harms those wearing them, as they have to continually breathe in their exhaled poisonous carbon dioxide.

Communist China masterminded this pandemic in response to the economic sanctions that had been placed on them for violating copyright laws, stealing intellectual properties and cheating on trade embargos. The Chinese government insisted a clause be in place that would prevent the sanctions from taking effect if a worldwide pandemic mysteriously broke out. The very next day, the first Chinese virus was discovered in North Korea. Then the next day, one case was discovered in America. The rest is history.

> *The Spirit of God has raised up the One New Man who has healing wings that carry curative, restoring light rays in his hands.*

There are communist, deep state globalist and socialist powers that will feed the media their fear tactics in order to panic and control the world's population. They will use any diabolical measure necessary to force the free world to conform to their one world religion—all gods being equal and one world currency system of buying and selling—until we lose all of our religious, social, economic, political and moral freedoms. No one wants to be transformed into a mindless, robotic clone that follows a tyrannical, communist government or Muslim directive.

The Spirit of God has raised up the One New Man who has healing wings that carry curative, restoring light rays in his hands. When this miracle healing anointing is released in public places, like churches, parks, beaches and stadiums, everyone who is in attendance will be healed by God's amazing grace.

God, I've heard what our ancestors say about you, "His brightness was like the light! He had rays flashing from His hand, and there His power was hidden." I have heard Your audible voice and I was afraid stopped in my tracks, trembling down on my knees. Revive Your work in the midst of these years make Yourself known but, in Your wrath, please remember mercy. His glory covered the heavens, and the earth was full of His praise. Do among us what you did among them. Work among us as you worked among them. And as You bring judgment, as You surely must, remember mercy.

God's on His way again, retracing the old salvation route, coming up from the south through Teman, the Holy One from Mount Paran. Skies are blazing with His splendor, His praises sounding through the earth, His cloud-brightness like dawn, exploding, spreading, forked-lightning shooting from His hand—what power hidden in that fist! Plagues flee as they march before Him, pestilence and fever fall at His heels! He stops. He stood and measured the earth; He surveyed the world and startled the nations. He shakes Earth. He looks around. Nations tremble. The age-old mountains fall to pieces; ancient hills collapse like a spent balloon.

I saw everyone worried, in a panic: Old wilderness adversaries, Cushan and Midian, were terrified, hoping He wouldn't notice them. The paths God takes are older than the oldest everlasting mountains that were scattered and the perpetual hills bowed down to His ways for they are everlasting (Habakkuk 3:2–6).

The Spirit of God is the only power that brings forth eternal transformation. Spiritual transformation requires a death to the old followed by a vision of resurrection that transitions us into a new life image. A new idea or concept is cast upon the imagination that then creates a gateway for that higher state of being to be manifested.

Whenever we live in the faith of God, believing that His Word is true, we literally become whatever the Word of God says we are and can become. *For as many as are led by the Spirit of God, these are Sons of God* (Romans

8:14). The Sons of God mature into the One New Man.

Believers see by the eyes of faith when they submit their whole being to the creative imagination of God. *But we all, with unveiled face, beholding as in a mirror the glory of the Lord, are being transformed into the same image from glory to glory, just as by the Spirit of the Lord* (2 Corinthians 3:18).

Transformation takes place when we die to self and transition into taking on the image of Christ, who has the power to break us out of our current limitations. We must be conscientious and full of the God kind of faith to believe what the imagination is showing us.

> *Spiritual transformation requires a death to the old followed by a vision of resurrection that transitions us into a new life image.*

Know that we are already the wise person of integrity in Christ. We have already taken on His character and attributes. Knowing this as fact qualifies us to emerge from our transformational cocoon and transition into a greater enlightened identity. It is the faith and mercies of God, not natural means, that empower us to sustain this new spiritual life in Christ, worshipping as living sacrifices dedicated to God.

> *I beseech you therefore, brethren, by the mercies of God, that you present your bodies a living sacrifice, holy, acceptable to God, which is your reasonable service. And do not be conformed to this world, but be transformed by the renewing of your mind, that you may prove what is that good and acceptable and perfect will of God* (Romans 12:1–2).

King Christ came to King Solomon

God asked Solomon what he wanted to receive in an imaginative dream. The Spirit of God does not come to discuss with us the step-by-step process of transformation; He comes to reveal the image and likeness we will walk in as an end result.

When we ask God for anything, we must ask in faith. We cannot waver in prayer. We must believe that we have already received what we have believed, seen and asked for. If we ask God from the position of already being in the likeness, image and nature of God's character, we will receive whatever we have asked in His name. But if we attempt to use the names of God as a mantra (an incantation) or conjure up His names like some magic spell, expecting positive results, nothing will happen.

King Solomon entered into a dialogue with God in the imaginative realm of vision. Solomon knew himself. He understood his current abilities, skills level and limitations. Solomon knew that unless God added His presence to him, he would not be able to go beyond his present level of knowledge, wisdom, understanding or seeing. Like King Solomon, Believers also have an unlimited access to God. We can obtain everything that was given to Solomon and so much more because we live under great grace, not law.

Because God is not a respecter of persons, every one of us can expect to receive dreams and visions, creative ideas, unique images, wisdom and visitations from the Spirit of God. The distant future can be drawn into our present life circumstances. We can transcend earthly limitations in order to transform the invitation that is seen in a vision form by bringing it into our reality.

> *As for you, my son Solomon, know the God of your father, and serve Him with a loyal heart and with a willing mind; for the Lord searches all hearts and understands all the intent of the thoughts. If you seek Him, He will be found by you; but if you forsake Him, He will cast you off forever* (1 Chronicles 28:9).

We can see and revisit visions that are hosted in the imaginative mind that have already become real to us. When we focus on becoming like these futuristic, visionary images, we are able to operate in the same transformational power that is found when we embraced the image of the end result.

The imagination empowers us to create a new identity and fresh purpose, and it empowers us to achieve our amazing destiny. By looking ahead and focusing on animating the future, we bring it into our present state of being. Our focused, faith-filled attention makes room that causes the increased grandeur of possibilities to settle into their resting place. Faith causes the acceleration of the arrival of future events that are destined to take place in our life.

Dreams come to search our heart, to reveal who we are at the current moment. But dreams also encourage us to change by revealing the greatness of who we are destined to become when we apply God's divine knowledge to our lives.

In a dream, King Solomon requested an understanding heart (the ability to hear God's voice) to obtain His knowledge and to understand divine wisdom. *You shall walk after the Lord your God and reverently fear Him, and keep His commandments and obey His voice, and you shall serve Him and cling to Him* (Deuteronomy 13:4). Solomon activated his imagination to see beyond the natural. King Solomon placed his focus on understanding the hidden depths within a person's heart to obtain God's supernatural endowments of comprehension, expertise and intelligence in order to lead a nation.

Nations are full of states that make up a kingdom. As citizens of the kingdom of heaven, we travel through different states to reach either a natural or spiritual destination. The United States of America is comprised of fifty different states. All of these geographic states continually exist, although we can physically live in only one state at a time. If we visit, move to, vacation in or travel to a different one of the fifty states, or if we decide to take up residence there, the previous state we left does not disappear or stop existing as part of the United States of America. Every individual state remains a present state, even when we are not a resident (dwelling in) that particular state at the moment. We can rest in, walk to, drive through or fly over every American state, but we can only dwell in one state at a time.

> Our focused, faith-filled attention makes room that causes the increased grandeur of possibilities to settle into their resting place.

I used the above anecdote to illustrate how we travel in the Spirit realm, with American states representing mansions or states of being. The awakened imagination has the ability to ascend or descend or to enter into or exit any of the eternal states of being that make up the infinitely expanding Kingdom of God. We live and move and have our state of being in Christ, who is our own beautiful imagination that resides within us.

We enter into different states of being when we experience various positive or negative attitudes, high or low emotions and productive or destructive thoughts. We move in and out of one geographic or spiritual state of being into another mansion or dwelling place. Wherever we focus our attention or spend our time thinking or talking about someone or something (those intellectual or emotional places where we continually dwell) is the state of being that we have taken up residence in for that time period in our life.

Sometimes when we experience a traumatic event, loss, grave disappointment or failure, we get stuck in a state of grief or take up residence in a hopeless state of depression or despair. One of the things we need to remember is that whether we are enjoying a positive state or lingering in a negative state, unless we transition, we will remain in that state. For all states are eternal.

These endless spiritual states of being were created before we were created. We do not create states on our own, but we choose to enter, dwell in or leave them according to our emotional thoughts, confessions, beliefs, actions or focused imagination. My words and thoughts may be true, but if I do not prophesy, pray and act on them in faith (becoming a doer of the word), the state I desire to occupy will not manifest. Our thoughts inspire the words that are like the gasoline that powers the engine of a car. The ideas of our imagination ignite the velocity and measure of the movement that propels the vehicle into forward motion (or an opposite or reverse direction). They cause the vehicle to speed into overdrive or cause it to idle at a standstill or stall out.

Faith causes the acceleration of the arrival of future events that are destined to take place in our life.

To be successful, we must learn the ways of God, then move when and how God moves. The Spirit of God (means *Messiah*) prepared, moved, hovered and brooded over the face of the waters to recreate the earth. Earth's face was without form, and an empty waste of deep darkness covered its surface (see Genesis 1).

In the wilderness, the nation of Israel learned to break camp, take up their tents and follow the movement of the cloud (the Spirit of Rising Truth) by day and the pillar of fire (progressive enlightenment through meditating on a profound truth) by night. To advance into a deeper truth or a greater level of spiritual enlightenment, I must pull up the ship's anchor in order to sail into unexplored horizons. I must sever the cords of the hot air balloon so it can freely ascend, arising to innovative heights as the new day dawns.

> *We should seek godly wisdom to acquire spiritual skills, prudence, good judgment and insightful perceptions.*

Solomon knew that in order to rule God's people effectively, he had to apprehend a supernatural ability to hear God's voice. To understand the ways of God's Spirit, Solomon had to gain a broader vision. We, like Solomon, have access to the mind of Christ. Believers have the ability to know All Things, to arise with God's answers to gain the revelation knowledge and power to heal society!

Because God is the eternal source of all states, both physical and spiritual, we can access all the states of glory, all the states of knowledge, all the states of wisdom and all the states of power through the mind of Christ, *"My hand made these things so they all belong to Me," declares Yahweh. "But there is one My eyes are drawn to: the humble one, the tender one, the trembling one who lives in awe of all I say"* (Isaiah 66:2).

Partnering with Christ, as a beloved son or daughter of God, empowers us to be a know-it-all and to have it all. By accessing God's wisdom, we can explore His knowledge of All Things. *So we are convinced that every detail of our lives is continually woven together to fit into God's perfect plan of bringing good into our lives, for we are His lovers who have been called to fulfill His designed purpose* (Romans 8:28).

The fear of the Lord is the beginning of wisdom. We should seek godly wisdom to acquire spiritual skills, prudence, good judgment and insightful perceptions. Wisdom is the principal thing we should seek. And in all of the states that we have already received from the Spirit of God, we should ask to receive the state of godly understanding, the state of spiritual discernment, the state of comprehension and the state of interpretation (see Proverbs 4:7).

King Solomon was considered wise. He knew that he needed God's wisdom and knowledge in order to be a successful king. Wisdom is to know thyself. Before I can truly know God or others, I need to know and love myself first. *O Lord, You, have searched me and known me* (Psalm 139:1).

God granted Solomon every state of being he asked for. All states of existence are always present and available; they never leave. We are the ones who transition in and out of or leave a certain state of existence. If we have ever entered any state of being or mansion, we can always return to rest in that attitude. Or we can depart from there to ascend or descend into another state of consciousness.

God also abundantly blessed King Solomon with many more states that he did not ask for. He granted Solomon the states of existence that would maintain a long life. He also gave Solomon fame, knowledge and wisdom while dwelling in the mansions of wealth, health, riches and honor. The imagination is more valuable than wealth, for with it we can create the future of All Things that exist in a higher mansion but not currently resting in our present life. *Therefore, I say to you, whatever* (states or mansions) *you ask when you pray, believe that you receive them* (those requested states or mansions), *and you will have them* (states or mansions) (Mark 11:24).

Manifesting a specific state of being requires us to have faith that believes we can enter into the door (Jesus). When we ask to know the Way, seek to know the Person of Truth and knock on the Eternal Door of Life, He (Jesus) will receive us unto Himself. No one can approach or gain access to the Father or take up residence in the Father's house unless Jesus opens the door or gives them

Believers feel the vibrations of God's glorious presence, experience His great mercy and thrive on the energy of His passion.

the keys (to those parts of the Kingdom of God) that grants them right of entry.

Once our imagination utilizes the kingdom keys to prayerfully open the stately mansion doors, we step up and move in. By clothing ourself with the majestic garments of that state, we take on the noble identity found in the splendor of revelation knowledge. And being objectively formed into the gracious images we see in this new mansion, we become a grand, new creature abiding in Christ. We have traveled in our imagination to access the places that Jesus had gone before us to prepare for us to live, move and have our being in. These places are the higher states of the innumerable mansions of the Father's house.

Like King Solomon, every time we awake from a dream, it is an invitation to be a new, regal, stately and noble person. We have been given a different, imposing spiritual perception. Taking on the dignified, visionary images in this august state fills us with godly wisdom and majestic knowledge. This releases a transformative power that magnifies and enhances our present state of being.

This out of this world wisdom connects us to all of heaven's glory and resources. Knowledge is described as an insight into the nature of anything that gives you an edge. Heavenly knowledge causes me to know God and to know who IAM called to be in Him.

> *"Now give me wisdom and knowledge that I may go out and come in before this people; for who can judge this great people of Yours?" Then God said to Solomon: "Because this was in your heart* (the inner man of imagination), *and you have not asked riches or wealth or honor or the life of your enemies, nor have you asked long life—but have asked wisdom and knowledge for yourself, that you may judge My people over whom I have made you king—wisdom and knowledge are granted to you; and I will also give you* (states and mansions of) *riches and wealth and honor, such as none of the kings have had who were before you, nor shall any after you have the like"* (2 Chronicles 1:10–12).

Believers feel the vibrations of God's glorious presence, experience His great mercy and thrive on the energy of His passion. We long for His warm embrace and the heat of His fiery, undying love. We hear the host of angelic languages when they join us in travail to birth the passionate, powerful presence of God's Kingdom on earth.

> *Now when Solomon had finished praying, fire came down from heaven and consumed the burnt offering and the sacrifices, and the glory of the Lord filled the house. The priests could not enter into the house of the Lord because the glory of the Lord filled the Lord's house. All the sons of Israel, seeing the fire*

come down and the glory of the Lord upon the house, bowed down on the pavement with their faces to the ground, and they worshiped and gave praise to the Lord, saying, "Truly He is good, truly His lovingkindness is everlasting" (2 Chronicles 7:–3).

We are living in the Church's greatest transitional era in history. Because we, as Believers, are the Church (the Bride of Christ), we must transition spiritually in order to release the transformational power to others.

Let Us Pray

Holy Spirit, You are the only power that exists who can bring forth eternal transformation. A transformation that requires a death to the old in order to follow a vision of resurrection that raises me up into a new existence, which transitions me into a new life image. Thank you that in Christ, IAM already the wise person of integrity who has taken on His character and attributes.

I ask that You give me a greater measure of faith so that I can sustain my new spiritual life in Christ. Make my body a living sacrifice that is holy and acceptable to God. Thank you for revealing the image and likeness that I will walk in as an end result. I believe that I have already received it; therefore, it is so.

Teach me how to enter into a spiritual life-changing dialog with You in my dreams. Activate my imagination so that I can see beyond the natural and obtain God's supernatural endowments of comprehension, expertise and intelligence. Teach me how to learn the ways of God so that I can move as the Spirit of God moves. Help me to seek you with all of my heart so that You are found of me. The fear of the Lord is the beginning of wisdom. I want to gain godly wisdom so that I can acquire spiritual skills and prudence and live a life full of good judgments. Amen.

CHAPTER FIVE

Spiritual Transition

The era of reformation has transformed Believers in Christ. We have transitioned from being a Church based on the doctrine of man's theology to being the Sons (and Daughters) of God. The Sons of God manifest His presence and usher in the revelation knowledge of the Kingdom of God in demonstration and power. The traditions of man that caused spiritual deafness have been removed, so Believers are able to hear the living Word of God and follow the voice of the Holy Spirit. By experiencing physical, tangible encounters with the God, we are moving from only knowing about God in theory (having heard about Him from what others have told us) to giving personal expression to His heart through our imaginations.

Kingdom Believers are trading in their old wineskins to receive new, flexible wineskins in order to advance past the basic milk (in the biblical fundamentals of the elementary things taught in the Word) to the mature meat, seasoned wine and heavenly manna. The Holy Spirit in us is breathing in the rhema Word of God so that we can imagine God's greatness and breathe out the Ruach manifestation of the realms of glory. Believers are discerning root causes of sickness, disease and moral decay in order to obtain the full fruitfulness of the working of miracles based in the acts of God's wisdom. We are moving from faith to anointing, from anointing to glory, from the entry level of glory to higher and exceedingly higher realms of endless expressions of glory.

Believers who know their God shall do great exploits. We are no longer *man pleasers* who are held captive by the fear of man or COVID-19. By embracing the reverential fear of the Lord, we have become *God pleasers.* Revelation comes to transform people and expand the Kingdom of God. The power of Christ Jesus dwelling in the imagination of man has the power to deliver humanity from ignorance, lack, boredom and the struggling existence of a poor self-image. The Christ within heals our broken states of personal, emotional, spiritual and literal poverty.

If man refuses to use his imagination, he will remain a common, ordinary person of sin, never knowing, understanding or reaching his God-given potential. *Then Jesus said to them, "When you lift up the Son of Man, then you will know that IAM He, and that I do nothing of Myself; but as My Father taught Me, I speak these things"* (John 8:28).

As Believers, we have been given access to the mind of Christ. Jesus thinks in the vast expanses of wisdom and in the unperceivable realms of revelation knowledge. *For I neither received it from man, nor was I taught it, but it came through the revelation of Jesus Christ* (Galatians 1:12).

The Law of Life in Christ Jesus brings an increased abundance, fullness and overflow. The promises of God will elevate a Believer's redeemed mind to think in a higher level of faith. Problems are not presented to defeat us; they increase or multiply our abilities. Problems promote us by stretching our current level of faith. Difficulties and pressure cause our faith to rise up and flow into the next dimension of glory in order to obtain God's supernatural wisdom and power to do the impossible.

> *Problems are not presented to defeat us; they increase or multiply our abilities. Problems promote us by stretching our current level of faith.*

When we enter into the spiritual realm that is able to accomplish the impossible, we have exchanged intellectualism for intimacy. The renewing of our mind enables our imagination to think higher (God-motivated) thoughts. The Holy Spirit continually removes the boundaries of natural limitations. God is limitless! We are created in God's image to arise beyond all conceived limitations, deliver ourselves and others, and reign the world.

Renew your mind with the washing of God's Word to think

higher thoughts; we have the mind of Christ. For who has known the mind of the Lord, that He will instruct him? But we have the mind of Christ (1 Corinthians 2:16).

Have you ever really thought about what it means to have the mind of Christ?

We must become skilled at resting in the intimacy found in Christ. These critical times in which we live require a different spiritual approach, higher thoughts and bold prophetic declarations, decrees and actions. We need to ask for and operate in great faith. This will empower us to discover and move into a new dimension of Christ consciousness. In this broader sphere of revelation, we gain a greater level of authority and an increased measure of the anointing that will cause our imagination to ascend into glory. *For as the heavens are higher than the earth, so are My ways higher than your ways and My thoughts* (imagination) *than your thoughts* (imagination) (Isaiah 55:9).

> When we enter into the spiritual realm that is able to accomplish the impossible, we have exchanged intellectualism for intimacy.

Spiritual unity empowers Believers to be filled with all the fullness of God. We learn how to tap into all the gifts, anointings, assets of glory and talents that are represented, present and currently available in the room. It requires all the saints compiling all of their gifted attributes together as one to know, experience and demonstrate the fullness of God's love. Spiritual synergy is powerful!

> *May we be able to comprehend with all the saints what is the width and length and depth and height—to know the love of Christ which passes knowledge; that you may be filled with all the fullness of God. Now to Him who is able to do exceedingly abundantly above all that we ask* (speak, pray, prophesy, decree) *or think* (imagine), *according to the power* (faith-focused attention) *that works in us* (Ephesians 3:18–20).

Thinking godly, imaginative thoughts causes us to change in various ways. Our newly-formed image produces more success not only in our personal, spiritual and social spheres but also in our business and ministry arenas.

Godly, imaginative thoughts will establish a broad foundation of stability in every area of our lives, which we can continue to build from. The Holy Spirit communicates the mind of Christ to us through heaven's open windows. All we have to do is to rest in His loving presence, surrender to His greater plans and accept His perfect will. The two-edged sword of the Lord comes down in a powerful way to both cut away things that would harm us and cut to heal us.

> Godly, imaginative thoughts will establish a broad foundation of stability in every area of our lives, which we can continue to build from.

No one can force change on you or anyone else. Most people will resist the power of force with an equal amount of opposite force. The only person you have the power to change is you. When you agree with God's higher plans for your life and change accordingly, others will notice, celebrate you and adjust their own behavior according to the measure that you have changed.

Whatever we think (imagine) upon, respond to, ask for, seek and talk about become our reality, our dwelling place or state of being. We always attract to ourselves what we already are, not who we want to become. To change the people and life circumstances that we attract, we must repent, pray and apply God's Word to change our thoughts, beliefs, inner speech and self-image. Whatever we can believe for, clearly see and boldly image will be. The imagination is our pioneering forerunner that sees the future and brings every possibility into our waking reality.

Personal Reflection Moment

1. Who is the new you that you want to birth?
2. What do you look and act like in the future?
3. What are your new desires?

When we agree with what God is saying, the words of our mouth will echo His greatness. When we mirror God, we will be transformed into His image and likeness from the inside out. When we become aware that the thoughts we think form our actions, we will be able to change and enhance the events of our lives.

Believers are learning strategic spiritual warfare that will draw a moral dividing line in the sand. Begin the change by becoming a voice that is creating a better world by praying, prophesying, decreeing and declaring the Word of God.

Let Us Pray

Dear Jesus, as I lift up the Son of Man, draw all men unto Yourself. Thank you for the access to the mind of Christ and the vast expanses of wisdom and revelation knowledge that is available to me. I embrace the law of life in Christ Jesus in order to increase in abundance, fullness and overflow. Empower me to have the strength that is necessary to accomplish the impossible, for I know that with You, God, nothing is impossible. Remove all of my natural boundaries of limitation, for You are limitless!

Teach me how to arise in the power of Your name and strength to deliver, save and reign upon this earth as it is in heaven. Renew my mind with the washing of God's Word to think higher thoughts. Teach me how to enter in and rest in the secret place of Your presence. Fill me with Your fullness. Help me to tap into all the gifts and talents that You have given me. Help me to be willing to be changed and transformed into Your likeness and image. Amen

CHAPTER SIX

Keys to Success

Imagine having the golden Midas touch of success that causes you to prosper in every endeavor you undertake or in every relationship. Imagine your name being listed alongside the titles of famous world leaders, the great men and woman of influence. Imagine you are a world changer, sought after for your wise advice that solves universal problems or heals incurable diseases *wisdom brings success* (Ecclesiastes 10:10).

> *This Book of the Law shall not depart from your mouth, but you shall meditate in it day and night, that you may observe to do according to all that is written in it. For then you will make your way prosperous, and then you will have good success* (Joshua 1:8).

Personal Reflection Moment

1. How do you define success?
2. Is success measured by the size of your bank account, the number of houses, property or corporations you own, the victories you've won or the problems you've solved?

> *Solomon finished the house of the LORD and the king's house; and Solomon successfully accomplished all that came into his*

> *heart to make in the house of the LORD and in his own house* (2 Chronicles 7:11).

3. Is success a loving marriage or a long-held, prosperous career?

4. Or is true success determined by the development of one's sterling character, full of love, and a positive, productive work ethic that helps others succeed as well.

5. Knowing that you cannot take anything tangible (property or the like) with you to heaven except the essence of your personality's nature, your character and your humanity, what kind or type of success do you want to be?

True success matures; it is cultivated, and it progresses by empowering you to achieve your chief aims in life while helping others achieve their life purposes as well. *The LORD was with Joseph, and he was a successful man; and he was in the house of his master the Egyptian* (Genesis 39:2). The presence of God's wisdom residing within, and His grace resting upon us, grants us favor and invitations to enter into the houses, governments and corporations of the rich and famous. The knowledge of God's ways empowers us to give them hope for a successful life by instilling vision to execute positive changes.

Our renewed spirit prayerfully draws to us the right people with the godly wisdom and resources we need. The pleasant personality of a delightful soul acts like a magnet that attracts our chief aims, our definite goals, our life purpose and the unwavering desires of our heart's *imagination* to us.

> *Always focus on finding the answers through the variety of solutions and possibilities. Never fixate on the problem.*

Have a specific, clear-cut chief aim and life purpose. A detailed plan will keep you from wandering aimlessly through life, serving everyone else's purposes instead of exerting your efforts on achieving your own goals.

Success means that you have learned how to trust God to help you overcome the basic fears in life by developing a real Christ-conscious knowledge that is based in genuine self-confidence. Success comes by knowing that Christ always has your best in mind. *And we know that All Things work together for good to those who love God, to those who are the called according to His purpose* (Romans 8:28).

Success is often stalled by the fear of disease and death. Success is deterred by poverty in old age from the lack of saving money during one's productive years. Success is also often mired by the disapproval of others and it's encumbered by heartache due to the loss of love.

Personal Reflection Moment

1. Are you aware of your weakness
2. Do you suffer from intolerance, greed, jealousy or suspicion?
3. Are you a vengeful person with a conceited ego?
4. Do you take credit for ideas you did not conceive or for work you did not do?
5. Do you live under the strain of debt because you spend more money than you earn?
6. Are you able to create a plan that will help you overcome any of these character flaws and bridge any gaps in your integrity?

   And He (Christ) *said to me, "My grace is sufficient for you, for My strength is made perfect in weakness." Therefore, most gladly I will rather boast in my infirmities, that the power of Christ may rest upon me* (2 Corinthians 12:9).

7. What parts of your life and personality do you need to transform in order to become a better person or a leader instead of a follower?
8. To be successful, you need to have the power to influence others that comes by accepting more responsibility when it is offered. Can you be trusted to always

do the right thing for all those concerned?

9. Are you able to concentrate your pleasant abilities on motivating people to cooperate with you in a spirit of harmony? Can you accurately separate important facts from random information to solve problems in a timely fashion?

Determine to achieve your top priorities one at a time. Be like a large cargo ship that breaks through life's barriers and all the crashing waves that try to hinder your progress. Know exactly what you want, and then courageously captain your ship. Set a straight forward course, which will barrel through any resistant obstacles, until you reach your destiny. Then dock the transport vessel in your safe harbor to both deliver and receive your bountiful rewards.

In order to be successful, we must consciously believe that we are successful! We can redefine the person we want to be by taking intentional actions to make it so. Setting strategic goals that will accomplish our destiny turns the knowledge we have gained into productive power. Knowledge becomes power when the counsel that is sought is wise enough to always tell us the truth, even if it is painful to hear and embrace at that moment. *The lips of the wise disperse knowledge, but the heart* (vain imaginations) *of the fool does not do so* (Proverbs 15:7).

> *To be successful and accomplish our goals, all we have to do is imagine and believe that it is workable with God.*

True knowledge, when placed in an organized motion, will bring forth harmonious improvements so that we can accomplish our purpose without violating the rights and expressions of others. If we are not living life to its fullest or working in a career that matches our potential, we are being idle. To be successful and accomplish our goals, all we have to do is imagine and believe that it is workable with God. So agree to do it together!

It is important to spend time stimulating the mind to imagine new ideas. But it is also just as important to review and update concepts, to develop different plans and strategies from old products or endeavors. This practice will create new income streams from new venues and markets that empower us to achieve our life goals, aims and desires. The mind has the power to picture images, create inventions, produce art and perceive wisdom found in philosophies that are suspended in the invisible Spirit realm waiting to be taught, yearning to be created and manifested.

Take time to reshape, improve, reinvent and release your previous thoughts and ideas. Think of ways to redesign and broaden the services you offer. Give your product lines a fresh appearance.

Personal Reflection Moment

1. Can what you offer to the public be broadened into new market areas or be used in a different manner or for a new function?
2. Can your products be utilized for various purposes by assorted people or diverse organizations?
3. What is your main career goal or priority in life?
4. What do you hope to accomplish with the strength of the years you have been given?

It is helpful to list your relationships in the order of priority with your greatest desire first. Then focus on improving, developing and accomplishing each one by one. Remember, sometimes the anticipation of receiving a dream or thing is sweeter than its realization. If there is the continual hope of obtaining it as a future goal, satisfaction remains alive and endures the test of time. Once your goal is in hand, it no longer satisfies; it is time to enjoy the victory. Begin imagining a new project to develop.

Always focus on finding the answers through the variety of solutions and possibilities. Never fixate on the problem. If you like where you are, keep talking about it, build a house and live there. But if you want to do something different with your life, you must change by imagining the possibilities, thinking of your options, talking to those you care about and acting differently.

Organize your time, and allow your imagination to create structures and solutions. Focus your energy by concentrating your attention on one strategic aim at a time. Develop a simple plan to master that particular subject until you have fulfilled all of your heart's desires pertaining to that goal.

Cultivate an efficient team by being courteous and friendly. Coordinate your efforts and thoughts with others of like mind and intention. Invest your time and energy into those who work harmoniously together. When you bring an assembly of people together, learn to cooperate with others' efforts and ideas. Remember that their imaginative ideas have the power to make life easier and more exciting as well. Their added energy may spark solutions you have not thought of that will help accomplish your goals.

Listen to the diverse input and controversial ideas of others in order to broaden your reasoning skills. Listening (while using wisdom and godly discernment of whether or not to accept their ideas as truth) will help eliminate all competition, jealousy, envy and strife. Rid yourself of all the negative friction caused by strife, envy, jealousy and greed. Rejoice when others succeed. Do not be suspicious or seek revenge when others wrong you. In its place, forgive, bless and pray for them. Change the critical, negative way you view others, and they will take on a different air around and toward you.

Uncooperative, negative, critical, doubt-filled people wreak havoc within a group. They devour team unity by causing dissension and division. They often create an atmosphere that fosters an unhealthy competition. Selfish vying handicaps production, making any forward motion difficult. Divisive actions are like trying to gain access to a super highway while driving a vehicle with square wheels. *A fool despises his father's instruction, but he who receives correction is prudent* (Proverbs 15:5).

> *When you bring an assembly of people together, learn to cooperate with others' efforts and ideas.*

The highest form of respect and admiration is to decree you will maintain truth between friends forever. Learn how to prosper from others' critical opinions. *The ear that hears the rebukes of life will abide among the wise* (Proverbs 15:31).

Learn to be tolerant of others. Be accessible to listen to their political ideas. Learn how to profit from knowing about their religious differences. Avoid being prejudice of people in order to keep an investigative door open that will produce a path for more fruitful communication. Religious and political intolerance, racial mistrust or cultural prejudice promote fear, suspicion and misgivings. They make enemies of those who should be friends.

Opportunities surround us on every side. They are easily found when we open our eyes to see from a different prospective. The ignorantly blind man closes the book of opportunity on the input and ideas of others, those who could be friendly assets, simply because they are unfamiliar and feel different. The vision of our natural eyes sees things in a distorted manner, believing opportunities to be so near that it causes fear or believing possibilities to be so farsighted that it causes doubt. The imaginative eyes focus on the leading of the Spirit always seeing with perfect, 20/20 clarity every time.

> *Fear paralyzes progress, prevents new opportunities and destroys initiative.*

Practice harmony by applying the Golden Rule: Do unto others as you would have them do unto you! Learn to prefer others above yourself. Remember, it is not always about you!

Develop self-confidence, knowing that through Christ nothing is impossible for those who believe. The love of Christ will conquer all forms of fear.

Learn to faceoff and defeat the fear of failure, the fear of death, the dread of public speaking, the fear of rejection, disapproval or criticism and the fear of the loss of love. *A scoffer does not love one who corrects him, nor will he go to the wise* (Proverbs 15:12).

To lose someone you love is much better than never having loved him or her at all. Don't allow the fear of the death of a relationship cause you to miss out on a full, prosperous life with that special someone. Take chances on people, and explore new areas. Learn to grow in and through adversity.

Fear paralyzes progress, prevents new opportunities and destroys initiative. Learn to develop your self-confidence until you have a sound mind that supplies you with the necessary knowledge that conquers, overcomes and removes all fear. Know yourself—how much you know and don't know. Remember, most of what we fear never happens, because fear is born out of untrue beliefs.

If you fear that you will fail, you already have. If you are afraid to try, you won't. If you desire to win but think you can't, you have already lost your chance. If you think you will lose, you have already lost your motivation to try.

Make it your purpose to study and improve yourself until you become the top leader in your chosen field of expertise. Do not settle for being a follower. Be the one who sets the mark by always achieving your goal and constantly raising the standard.

Always take the initiative to be a kind, generous, supportive leader that unites the group by encouraging people through the use of suggestion, not by lording over them by force. Always look to find new ways to thank and empower the gifted team of people God has put together. He has sent them to help empower you, to complete every good work and to do His will, which pleases Him (see Hebrews 13:2).

Apply yourself and accept responsibility when it is offered. Learn how to rule in your chosen field or endeavor. A leader with a pleasing, intelligent, gracious personality will transform any situation into a positive working environment, where everyone can prosper harmoniously.

Honor is given to those who think long-term, who are always responsible to do the right thing and who uphold the highest of principles and their actions are rooted in a firm godly foundation.

We are capable of positive changes that bring success when we act responsibly by taking time to reason intelligently, then we choose to take a different or higher life path. Taking responsibility for our own choices causes others to develop trust in our character. They learn that we are dependable and accountable to those for whom we work. It is not easy to find people who are self-starters.

It is easy to treasure an employee who has built a good reputation as a problem solver, who is faithful and is self-motivated by internal convictions and ethics. *A faithful employee is as refreshing as a cool day in the hot summer time* (Proverbs 25:13). Honor is given to those who think long-term, who are always responsible to do the right thing and who uphold the highest of principles and their actions are rooted in a firm godly foundation. They live by their personal beliefs, and often simply enjoy the feeling of accomplishment that achieving another goal brings to them. These are focused, trustworthy individuals are of great value, and they make a difference wherever they go.

One of our greatest assets is our organized mind working in harmony with others toward a common goal. Leaders must possess patience, persistence, self-confidence, adaptability and poise. All of these positive assets empower people to impart the knowledge that can change circumstances without showing any annoyance, frustration, friction or anger.

> *Leaders must possess patience, persistence, self-confidence, adaptability and poise.*

Our self-confident poise and leadership skills reflect on our expert abilities. These positive attributes make us a successful, sought after person of prosperity. Do not let fame or success go to your head. Resist being conceited and egocentric. Ally and cooperate with others who possess the knowledge you need to tap into and harness.

Develop an enthusiastic personality. Be excited and expectant when sharing about your business or ministry. Influence others in your community or work force by encouraging them to cooperate with your ideas when meeting new people. Enthusiasm makes you unforgettable and your ideas contagious.

Develop a warm, inviting, pleasing personality that outshines the rest of your competition. Overcome environmental obstacles with a pleasant attitude that can adjust in a positive, helpful manner in order to assist, defuse or dominate any other personality type. People appreciate when you truly help them help themselves.

Many people never experience the changes that are needed. They are often too busy fighting against outer circumstances and building a wall to protect the inner cause found within the heart of their own imagination. People want to be rescued and redeemed, but they do not want to go through the necessary changes or processes that would improve them. Those who are willing to die to their present self (by taking on a higher image and standard of excellence) will be able to achieve every one of their life goals.

To expand the scope of our horizon, influence and income pool, we need to branch out to include a more diverse set of people from different walks of life. Render more services, and do a better job than you are expected to do. Offer more than you are being paid for. This will increase the monies that you will receive through repeated customers, those returning to your business.

Success begins in the mind, and victorious achievements are sustained in the dedicated heart of the imagination. Like magnets, we draw and harmonize with people who share our same character, thoughts, beliefs and life energy.

Personal Reflection Moment

1. To what kind of people are you attracted?
2. With whom do you surround yourself?
3. Are the relationships you draw unto yourself beneficial, life-giving and encouraging?

The person who wins the race is the person who believes in his imagination or her heart that he or she can and will succeed. If you think someone is better than you, they are. Learn to think well of yourself in order to rise above every obstacle. Build up and edify others with creative, sincere, loving words that magnify their good attributes. The release of joy is needed to produce a strong, secure person, who will be your loyal, adoring and lifelong friend.

Demand success for yourself, and then back it up with prayer and intelligent actions. Faith without works is dead. Success is the ability to positively adjust the environment by correcting the variances of society according to a godly, moral, just code of conduct. Permanent success comes when one is willing to look at him or herself in the mirror. Asking God for the wisdom to discover the root causes of his or her feelings or mistakes is the next step. He or she can then sincerely repent and graciously right all of his or her wrongs.

Your imagination is the mirror that reveals your soul, the person who you are currently. Your personal imaginative mirror also shows and reflects the person you desire to be by displaying who you are destined to become. It is important to take time to imagine all the possibilities of who and what you are able to become. A creative imagination produces fresh ideas that will enhance, renew and perfect your current plans. The imagination creates, births and releases our full potential to demonstrate all we were born to be.

To become a hero, one must conduct his or her life in a heroic manner. He or she must use past mistakes as steppingstones to empower a future platform of success. Learn to organize the knowledge you have received from overcoming your temporary failures so that disappointments remain just momentary, short-term delays, never a permanent defeat.

Failure is only a brief defeat that teaches vital life lessons to those who have eyes to see their botches as only a transient setback. To them, the knowledge that is gleaned becomes a hidden blessing that, when planted within their heart, takes root, grows, blooms and bears the sweet fruit of prosperity. The person who never makes a mistake is the same person who never takes a risk. Therefore, they achieve nothing of any significance in life. Look within to discover your chief heart's desire, then imagine who you will become when you make it your primary purpose or aim in life.

> *Permanent success comes when one is willing to look at him or herself in the mirror.*

To achieve success, one's personality must have developed the proper balances between the uses of the powers to influence people in a positive, productive and harmonious manner. One must be self-controlled, patient and long-suffering in order to master his or her destiny. One must also be willing to skillfully assist others in reaching their destiny as well.

Because people with full, productive schedules know how to get things done in an orderly, efficient fashion, they are sought out to do more. The virtue of self-control brings an equalized balance to your life's journey, which keeps you energized, stable and well-rounded.

Don't fear opposition or competition; soar to the top by mastering the multidirectional winds of adversity that seem to hit at the same time. Learn to rise to the highest levels of success, while standing against the hostility of your opponent's antagonism. Difficulties only make you stronger. Decide to use life's problems and complex troubles to your advantage.

The grass always appears greener on the other side of the fence. A mountain always looks majestically beautiful and awe-inspiring from a distance. It is not until you stand at its base that you realize the mountain is just a bunch of sand and rocks. To get to the other side of the mountain, we have to climb over or burrow through it to advance. The Bible encourages the Believer to speak to the mountain, plucking it up and casting it into the sea. *Whoever lives a life of honest integrity and says to this mountain, "Be uprooted, lifted up and thrown into the sea," and does not doubt at all in his heart but trusts and believes that what he says will take place, it will be done for him* (Mark 11:23).

When the imagination is content, it is because it is dwelling on thoughts of peace, beauty and happiness. Continue to focus on being gratified until you are able to capture your hope by bringing that distant vision or desired home to rest within your own heart. No one can buy a home, but it's easy to purchase a house. Homes must be carefully created with patience and a pleasing, loving touch that brings the warmth of a comfortable safe zone—a place where people are happy and free to relax and be who they were created to be.

Let Us Pray

Dear Jesus, You hold all the keys to the Kingdom of God. I believe IAM successful because You say IAM successful in You! The knowledge You have given me empowers me to accomplish my destiny in You. I choose to magnify You by keeping my eyes focused upon You, the answer to every problem, instead of fixating on the problem. Help me to always be efficient, courteous and friendly so that I can coordinate my efforts to be more productive with like-minded people. Help my mind to be content in my thoughts of You until I can bring that distant vision or God-given desire home to rest within my heart. Amen.

CHAPTER SEVEN

Free Will Choices

Imagination comes first before the state of belief can be manifested, so always imagine the grandest thing possible for yourself and others. If you have to insist that people treat you like a lady or gentleman, you may not be acting like one. Honoring the power of choice that is held by others does not diminish your own measure of power to choose, but it does make an opportunity for your measure of power to increase and change.

Free will grants us the freedom to choose the manner of how we think about and relate to ourself and others. Free will also affords us the opportunity to change the way we view people, the things we believe about them and what we express to others about them. Undesirable people will devalue you, diminish your image, drive you nuts, destroy your dreams, discourage and disbelieve your imagination, discredit your gifted abilities and doubt your opinions. Avoid pessimists at all cost.

From the beginning of civilization, oppressive dictators have accepted the rule of power and decision-making responsibility over the majorities. Their narrow-minded ways lead to socialistic bondage of poverty and slaughter. We, the majority, gave up our power of choice by remaining silent, doing nothing and never praying for deliverance.

Power-hungry people create a revolution in order to seize power as a dictator. Power is a means to an end, and they never relinquish control. The object of fear is fear, the object of terror is terror, and the object of persecution is persecution; there are no hidden agendas.

Evil oppressors control masses of people by repeating lies so often that the people regard them as truth. Where there is a misuse of power, there must be an equal amount of resistance. The aim of those who lie is to corrupt good manners by manipulating a person's belief in truth, justice, righteousness and holiness.

When power corrupts someone, it can be difficult to determine who is the villain and who is the real hero. One fights for justice, equality and the rights of others, while the other takes all rights from others for himself.

If people are able to change, then we are able to change the way we think about them. If I and others can change, then the negative way that we currently view them is not really the truth about them. The Bible warns us to not spread false reports (see Exodus 23:1). The Bible clearly states that whatever a person sows, he or she will also reap. If we gossip or lie about or slander or bear false witness against others, the evil harm we sought to bring on them will be executed against us.

If we choose to only imagine the good and positive potential in people, we will always decree and prophesy their highest destiny into being.

> *The judges must make a thorough investigation, and if the witness proves to be a liar, giving false testimony against a fellow Israelite, then do to the false witness as that witness intended to do to the other party. You must purge the evil from among you* (Deuteronomy 19:18–19).

If we harbor unforgiveness in our hearts and imagine vain things toward others, we will be turned over to the tormentors of the night. *Do not turn me over to the desire of my foes, for false witnesses rise up against me, spouting malicious accusations* (Psalm 27:12).

Honesty is always the best policy. An honest witness tells the truth, saves lives and does not deceive, but a false witness tells lies, is deceitful and stirs up conflict in the community (see Proverbs 6:19; 12:7; 14:5; 14:25). Those who spread lies in order to destroy a good reputation will eventually reap the consequences of what they have done. Rest assured, the corrupt people with whom a liar keeps company will also turn and devour him or her in due time. *A false witness will not go unpunished, and whoever pours out lies will not go free but will be punished* (Proverbs 19:5, 9).

The grace of God empowers us to see people at their best possible moment. If we choose to only imagine the good and positive potential in people, we will always decree and prophesy their highest destiny into being. *A good man out of the good treasure of his heart brings forth good; and an evil man out of the evil treasures of his heart brings forth evil. For out of the abundance of the heart's imagination his mouth speaks* (Luke 6:45).

If we view someone in a negative manner, we steal his or her creative potential. We lock that person in a prison of narrow limitation. Because we hold them captive in the dungeon of our own critical judgment, we stop their ability to evolve higher.

Our beliefs direct the things that happen in our lives. For example, if I think or assume that someone desires to harm or reject me, my subconscious imagination receives those thoughts as my truth. My imagination then goes to work to create that negative scenario within my mind. These sabotaging, wrong assumptions and perceptions give my negative, destructive thoughts the opportunity to manifest. Once they are birthed, they quickly grow until they appear as a riotous mob invading the scene. My own harmful thoughts flood into my world as my reality. Remember, we always get what we think, say, focus on, sow and expect to happen.

> The perception of IAM means that I have already discovered and agree with God's decree of who IAM in Christ.

Our assumptions convince us to believe as facts the ideas that we have conjured up about another. Once this happens, we tend to relate to and later live by our personal beliefs, as he or she has grown to become conformed to our own reality we hold.

We cannot change the negative notions we believe about an individual on our own. We must seek the Father's will about the individual and situation in order to repent of our negative attitudes. Then we need to properly pray, prophesy and decree into his or her life as God commands in order to change matters. To bring things into an appropriate relationship, we must move from believing that eventually something will happen in the future (*Someday I will be....* or *Someday I will do....* You fill in the blanks!) to believing that it is already accomplished or done now! When we take on this futuristic someday stance, it means that it is not ever going to happen. We must decree, believe and prophesy in the *now*!

By assuming a *now* faith position of being conscious of the Father's will for me, I have already assumed the position of IAM currently who the Father says IAM to be in the future. When I assume this position of faith (that IAM already), IAM believing, IAM receiving and IAM actively being the new identity now!

The perception of IAM means that I have already discovered and agree with God's decree of who IAM in Christ. IAM being the person God created me to be. IAM doing the Father's business by being who He says IAM. When we adopt a different concept of ourselves, we evolve into that new identity. By becoming a different person with fresh ideas, desires and a brand new, powerful image, we are able to give God the glory that is due His name.

> By changing our conscious awareness of our own being, we amend and correct the way we relate to the Father's will.

As eternal, spiritual beings, we have been given the creative powers that allow us to pick and choose who we were, who we are currently and who we will be in the future present. We choose what we will and will not do in life. When we take on a new identity in Christ, we alter the decisions we make. These Christlike choices cause us to be elevated to a higher path, which offers different options that have the power to positively revise life. By changing our conscious awareness of our own being, we amend and correct the way we relate to the Father's will. God grants us new doors of access and many more windows of opportunity. We can imagine and observe the myriads of fresh possibilities that can be ours if we so choose.

By simply reworking our self-concept to become a nobler one, we are interjected into a promising world of unlimited potential. We exchange our present world for a prosperous future of well-being in a higher, larger mansion. To prosper in a supernatural manner, it is important to place the visions that are created by reading the Word of God into your imagination. Once these visions are imagined, they can be remembered. They have become a memory of an already happened event. It is necessary to prayerfully reflect on these images until they become your tangible reality.

Personal Reflection Moment

> Confess: IAM an imaginative, speaking spirit with a creative voice who prophesies the Word of God! IAM an eternal, life-giving spirit who is confident and loving, and IAM secure in God. When I call on God, He always answers me with the grace of His wisdom, power and provision. I give all my problems to Him. I roll my personal concerns over onto God because He cares for me. My God-centered faith makes a way for the answers I need to enter through the powerful revelatory gates of the imagination through prayer, dreams, visions or trances. When IAM in the presence of God, I believe that He is able to do All Things—raise the dead and call into being things that do not currently exist in my present life. Amen!

We must choose to continually host God in a state of holiness, or we will remain a hostage to the strength of our own bloated pride and fragile ego. We become what we think, so carefully guard the thoughts of your imagination and the intents of your heart with all diligence.

> *Arise, cry out in the night, at the beginning of the watches; pour out your heart like water before the face of the Lord. Lift your hands toward Him for the life of your young children, who faint from hunger at the head of every street* (Lamentations 2:19).

The subconscious does not seek to change the conscious, but she longs for its intimate touch and interaction.

> *On my bed night after night* (I dreamed that) *I* (subconscious) *sought the one whom my soul loves; I desperately sought*

Him but did not find Him (consciousness). *I said, "His absence was so painful. So, I* (subconscious) *must arise now and go out into the city; hunting Him in the streets, alleys and into the squares* (places I do not know). *I must seek Him whom my soul loves." I wanted my lover in the worst way! I sought Him looking high and low, but I did not find Him. The watchmen who go around the dark city found me as they patrolled, And I said, "Have you seen Him, my dearest lost love whom my soul seeks?" Scarcely had I passed them when I found Him whom my soul loves. I threw my arms around Him and I held Him tight and would not let Him go until I had brought Him* (consciousness) *home again safe to my mother's house, and into the intimate chamber of her* (subconscious) *who conceived me* (Song of Songs 3:1–4).

During the night, the conscious mind returns to his lover (the subconscious) to process all of his feelings, to give expression to his desires and to share the things his senses have experienced during the day. *Would not God search this out? For He knows the secrets of the heart* (Psalm 44:21).

The fear of the Lord is the beginning of wisdom. *I applied my heart* (imagination) *to know, to search and seek out wisdom and the reason of things, to know the wickedness of folly, even of foolishness and madness* (Ecclesiastes 7:25).

For out of the issues of the heart (imagination) flows the abundant life. *Then I will give them one* (divine imagination) *heart, and I will put a new spirit within them, and take the stony heart out of their flesh, and give them a heart of flesh* (Ezekiel 11:19).

Skillfully choose the words of both your inner and outer conversations; they will frame your waking world. The subconscious longs for, will chase after, embrace, hold onto, bring home, conceive a pregnancy, incubate, grow, mature and give birth to whatever the conscience shows and tells her. Therefore, do not allow yourself to think on or constantly talk about the past or things that are currently missing in your life. All

> Giving thanks from a grateful heart has the power to create, attract and multiply the new things we desire.

that does is magnify lack and poverty. Instead, place your focused attentiveness on giving thanks to God for the positive things you already have in your possession. Giving thanks from a grateful heart has the power to create, attract and multiply the new things we desire.

Let Us Pray

Dear Lord Jesus, help me to imagine the grandest possible destiny that You have chosen for me. Cause me to think the best of people and relate to others in the manner that You see them. Let me always sow goodness, mercy and grace toward others. Let me keep a short list of offenses so that I walk in continual forgiveness of those who hurt or wrong me in anyway. Let me be an honest witness who always tells the truth, even to my own hurt. Empower me to make Christlike choices so that I can be elevated onto a higher, narrower path that leads to spiritual excellence.

Thank You for the new doors of opportunity to advance and for the blessing You have poured out on me from the windows of heaven. Teach me what it is to fear and revere You. Let the words of my heart and the conversations I hold reflect Your love. Let me always be thankful for the countless blessings You have lavished on me. Amen.

CHAPTER EIGHT

For Such a Time as This

Father Abraham manifested his desires through learning the art of prayerful thanksgiving to God as his source. Being of an advanced, mature age did not mean that Abraham had to be weak or in pain or to be infirmed, arthritic or diseased. Knowing that God is our eternal source causes us to come into His transformational presence with praise, singing, worship and thanksgiving to obtain everything we need.

Thankfulness causes us to come into harmony with God's creative powers. We are able to receive and manifest God's goodness and magnificent presence. Always anticipate and make room for the manifestation of God's greatness. Never react to the carnal nature; it is enmity against God. Be careful to only act on the God-given, positive thoughts and Holy Spirit impressions, aspirations and blessings.

To affect change in your life, enter into a time of rest to love, adore and seek the face of the Christ who lives within you. Thank Christ for sharing His creative ideas, facts, concepts and powerful spiritual insights with you. Think on, meditate on and contemplate His glory, excellent greatness and grandeur. Reflect, focus on and analyze the images that Christ produces within your soul until they fully emerge and come to rest in your spirit. Organize your images and ideas into a working plan. Develop a productive strategy that will bring them step-by-step into a manifested reality.

Evaluate, sort and then discern the difference between important and unimportant information, and separate them. Discern valuable facts in order to build a successful strategy and blueprint to obtain your future. Remember, your future is not being created; it already exists just waiting for you to discover how to choose and then implement your future's highest form.

Facts empower you to demonstrate your intelligent efforts by harmoniously organizing your knowledge in a productive manner. The more you know about God and His ways, the better and clearer your future will become.

God knows the number of days you will spend on earth. His infinite wisdom also knows the events He has predestined for your life. As you evolve in wisdom and love, you ascend onto a higher path of godly access. This improves your life by the excellent choices you make and decisive actions you take.

> *The more you know about God and His ways, the better and clearer your future will become.*

When we decide what we really want out of life, we learn to concentrate our attention on deliberately achieving that goal one step at a time. Therefore, time is one of the most valuable commodities in the world. Time affords us the power to correct the mistakes and temporary setbacks and to prevent them from permanently defeating us.

Time is the great equalizer. Everyone is given the same amount of time in every day. Therefore, if time is handled correctly, it has the power to right the wrongs of injustices. With the proper use of time and wisdom, nothing is impossible. The imagination is boundless, so imagine with all your mind. Desire justice and righteousness, believing it is so with all your heart. Decide it's possible to achieve, and then with all of your might, create the Kingdom of God on earth.

> *Not that I have already attained, or am already perfected; but I press on, that I may lay hold of that for which Christ Jesus has also laid hold of me. Brethren, I do not count myself to have apprehended; but one thing I do, forgetting those things, which are behind, and reaching forward to those things which are ahead, I press toward the goal for the prize of the upward call of God in Christ Jesus. Therefore, let us, as many as are ma-*

ture, have this mind and if in anything you think otherwise, God will reveal even this to you. Nevertheless, to the degree that we have already attained, let us walk by the same rule, let us be of the same mind (Philippians 3:12–16).

To adequately manifest God to the world, we must passionately adhere to our desired goals with a specific end aim in mind. Staying focused on completing one goal at a time keeps us from aimlessly wandering through barren deserts. It keeps us from carelessly drifting away on every wave that causes us to lose sight of God's plans to prosper our life.

The things that are being revealed from heaven will not be shaken. Because revelation is from the Kingdom of God, it will remain for eternity. His mandates are *for such a time as this!* Submit yourself to the will of God by peacefully resting in His presence. Recognize the greater working power of Christ that is living within you. Let your imagination produce a redemptive image of the person you desire to be coming forth, being created and resurrecting in your mind's eye. See yourself being sought out by those who once pushed you to the side or rejected you.

Time and the passage of years is not what change us. When the spirit understands God's love, it becomes aware of its ability to respond to God differently. As we adopt God's love, changes take place. We react in love instead of defending ourselves.

As Believers, we are called to be noble imitators of God, walking in His extravagant love. We are to avoid the unfruitful works of darkness, fornication, all sexual immorality, uncleanness, covetousness, lust and greed in order to inherit the Kingdom of God. Filthiness, foolish talking and coarse jesting are not fitting for a Christian. Jesus warns us to guard our speech and forsake obscenities and worthless insults. We are warned not to be disobedient or deceived by empty words. When we rise up from entertaining the dead works of the flesh, the Christ in us will shine His light through us. We are to walk circumspectly, not as fools but as wise people who know how to redeem the time in these days of evil (see Ephesians 5).

Choose your words carefully! If your words are harsh or critical, they will cut like knives and stab the very people God sent to help assist your assigned advancement. The words you speak frame, build, create and sustain, or they tear down and destroy your world. *Through or by faith we under-*

stand that the worlds were framed and prepared by the Word of God, so that things which are seen were not made of things which are visible and do appear (Hebrews 11:3).

Consistency brings productive change and new opportunities when you understand that it is the essentials of God's ways that empower you to achieve good success. Learn to prioritize according to biblical principles of wisdom. Remove and discard from your life whatever is not needed or useful for your spiritual advancement. We cannot bring the old ways and patterns into the new era. We must evolve into a higher order and adapt a standard of excellence.

The Apostle Paul became like a chameleon. He adapted to the marketplace and changed to meet the various situations of life so that he could influence people from every walk of life and win some for Christ. We need to rearrange economic structures to prosper with the vision we have been given.

Believing the Spirit of Truth brings change in the soul. The act of obedience will bring eternal life and spiritual illumination to the hungry hearts that are in search of the living God. The Holy Spirit descends and rests upon the present truth of God's revealed revelation knowledge; it does not rest on the empty vacuum of man's philosophies. The Spirit of Truth enlightens us inwardly so that what is known in our intellect will experience a divine transfer in order to be illuminated within our spirit. The Spirit of Truth will lead and guide us into all truth, for man becomes what he focuses on and believes. We learn the ways and precepts of God when our mind is infiltrated with the Holy Spirit's revelation knowledge.

> With the proper use of time and wisdom, nothing is impossible.

The imagination is the part of us that houses the impressions of the Spirit of Christ. Part of living in God's truth is learning to forgive yourself and others on a daily basis. *Judge not, and you shall not be judged. Condemn not, and you shall not be condemned. Forgive, and you will be forgiven* (Luke 6:37).

The moral standards that God raises keep us stable so that we will not be conformed to the world as it shifts, crumbles and changes around us. Believers who are able to stay focused on manifesting their objectives in a positive, creative manner, knowing that All Things are possible with God, will be able to achieve their desired results.

Undivided Attention

We have all heard someone say, "Pay attention to what I am saying." This means they want our undivided, focused attention trained on them. When doctors use a laser to cut out a tumor or to heal during surgery, they are using a machine that concentrates a large beam of light down into a fine cutting point. The laser condenses it into a very narrow, focused light that flows through a small, precise opening. When we become serious about making changes to our life, we will focus our attention on a specific outcome or one single concept, or we will develop one major idea at a time.

To be focused means that we see, hear, think and speak only of this one desire until it manifest as a fact of reality. We act as if we are obsessed with obtaining this one desire. When we want something to appear, we should eat, sleep, dream and talk about that desire with God. Our one desire should be God! He should be our first, primary aspiration, our foremost obsession in life; for within Him, All Things exist, live, move and have their being (see Acts 17:28).

As we seek the Kingdom of God first, we aim to please God and strive after all of His righteousness. We seek to know the way He does things and focus on His reality and initiative. If we do this, all of God's provisions will be added to us (see Matthew 6:33).

Creative power is released to the degree that we continue to focus our attention upon obtaining our God-given goals, desires, purpose and destiny. Likewise, success is determined by the degree we are able to focus our attention on achieving our aims in life.

Consistency brings productive change and new opportunities when you understand that it is the essentials of God's ways that empower you to achieve good success.

Sometimes our thoughts continually wander like a herd of feral cats that are trying not to be corralled. Learn how to patiently draw your thoughts back into a disciplined focus. Do not entertain habitual, negative thoughts. Never rehearse or recite harmful phrases.

Take time to practice using your imagination to redesign the image of yourself. See yourself as the ultimate person who can manifest a higher, more confident self that is fashioned in the loving image and beautiful likeness of God. The true test of the appropriate use of your imagination is determined by the residual outcome you receive from your focused thoughts and desires.

Personal Reflection Moment

1. Are you able to effectively focus your attention on achieving your goals in life?
2. What are the attitudes that you project toward yourself?
3. Are you your own greatest fan and supporter, or are you your chief, destructive critic?

Faithfully focus the attention of your imagination upon positive, creative, life-giving influences. Abandon yourself to God's transformational processes. The Almighty Trinity, formed of the Father, Jesus the Son and the Holy Spirit, is always unified in agreement as one amalgamated being, God.

Let Us Pray

Dear Jesus, teach me how to be thankful so that I can come into harmony with God's creative powers. I want to receive and manifest Your magnificent presence to demonstrate Your goodness. Thank You for sharing Your creative ideas and spiritual insights with me. Help me discern between facts and information that is important and that which is irrelevant. Teach me Your ways so that I can clearly see my future resting in You. In Your great wisdom, You have numbered my days. May they be fully pleasing unto You in every way. Help me to concentrate on fulfilling the plans and desires You have for me. I know that I AM inheriting an eternal kingdom that cannot be shaken.

Empower my imagination to see the redemptive image of the person You desire for me to be. Let me always respond in love, and let me never react in anger by defending myself to others. Help me to remain pure from all sexual immorality, uncleanness, covetousness, lust and greed so that I may inherit the Kingdom of God. Help the words of my mouth be full of love, grace and mercy. Amen.

CHAPTER NINE

Focused Faith

Our focused attention is developed through the constant exercise of our faith. When we practice living life by faith, the beliefs to which we hold will form a habitual path. Our godly convictions transform spiritual images, visions and dreams into our tangible reality. God's presence shows us the superior path that will bring us a joyous, pleasurable life.

The advanced pathways of Believers appear when they are constantly pondering about the greatness of the Lord. Our eyes are open to see in the Spirit when we boldly stand in God's presence. God's love conforms us into the image of God, so we can follow in the ways of God. Walking in the good ways of God enlarges the scope of our influence. There is rest for our souls in God. On the just path of the righteous, there is no sting of death.

The Spirit of God is always counseling, instructing and teaching us how to prosper on the path of justice, knowledge and understanding. When we submit our imagination to God, in order to fulfill His purposes, we will behold beautiful visions of grandeur. By concentrating and lavishing our love on God, He is able to release the Holy Spirit's creative force through our imagination until all that we desire from Him is manifested. When love rules the imagination of our heart, we are able to dive into and thrive in the deep things of God.

Love builds a firm, fruitful foundation that invites us to ascend and progress into the secret mysteries found only in God. When love rules our heart, we no longer reside thither in the shallow pools, where we are continually being trampled underfoot in the mud puddles of life. The imagination possessed by love can be trusted with an unlimited line of more power, influence and glory. Without love, we are viewed as noise, a clanging cymbal or an intrusive interruption, in the realm of the Spirit. This happens because we have not learned to enter into the spirit through the peaceful nature and character of Jesus, who is love and the only legal door of access to God.

> *Our godly convictions transform spiritual images, visions and dreams into our tangible reality.*

The wise build upon Jesus, who is the true foundation stone of our sanctified imagination. Our wholeness is dependent upon the measure of integrity, character and right standing we possess in Christ. Faith in God's creative process removes any limiting beliefs. This allows us to boldly enter in and confidently exercise the realm of great faith.

> *By faith Moses forsook Egypt* (the world, the darkness of evil and other gods), *not fearing the wrath of the king* (seeing you as you desire to be, exercising the powers of environmental forces to change and ruling or reigning your current circumstances); *for he endured as seeing Him who is invisible* (faith manifests what you endure or persist in believing that it has already transpired) (Hebrews 11:27).

The force of faith empowers our desires to change by giving birth to another measure of Christ within us. When we recognize that additional characteristic of Christ's greatness dwelling within us, we are transformed into that particular image of Christ. Faith is the substance that connects us to the creative life force of God. Faith empowers us to bring what we believe and hope for out of the realm of the Spirit. Faith causes our focused desire to be seen in the spiritual realms of dreams and visions. Faith empowers us to draw the invisible into our reality through a proper interpretation, declarative prayer, decree and prophecy.

When we trust in God's present power, we can be still and know that He is God living in us. It is Christ who rises within us to manifest the hope of things not yet seen. Christ reveals things that are currently invisible to us, still waiting to be found, so that they can be displayed in the realms of glory.

From before time began, secrets have been safely hidden in Christ, just waiting there for us to find them. By walking in God, we discover that we have the ability to hear, feel, see and intimately experience and know God. So in seeing, we are able to take on the position of our answers to prayer by simply believing and becoming what we see. Knowing that we have already been given the answer to our prayer request, we can easily receive it by faith. By us emulating God's kind of faith, we ignite a creative motion that instantly transfers and manifests the answers to prayer into our present state.

Focused faith empowers us to join with and manifest the things we desire or hope for, giving the invisible, spiritual truths a grand entrance into our visible, material life. Having seen, received and been clothed in a new mantle, we learn to wear and own this new garment of identity.

Do not be satisfied with just having faith in God. We must grow in faith until we have the faith of God. A seed must fall to the ground and die all alone. But if it dies, it will also resurrect into God's powerful, creative faith. It is faith that makes the prevailing Word of God alive, active, potent and productive in our flesh. The commanding faith of God empowers God to dwell in and among us.

> *Love builds a firm, fruitful foundation that invites us to ascend and progress into the secret mysteries found only in God.*

The mustard seed, although it is very small, always produces a mustard tree. A mustard seed represents the conscious, absolute, sure faith of God. The parable of the mustard seed demonstrates to the Believer that faith is true, producing a manifestation of whatever it is steadfastly focused upon. In Mark 4:31–32 and Matthew 13:31–32, the mustard seed is considered the least of all seeds. But when it (the conscious faith of God) is grown, it is the greatest among herbs. It becomes a tree that birds and animals can lodge in and under, where they can make their homes.

God is dealing with unbelief in the above referenced passages. The grain of mustard seed does represent faith, but it is not about the small size of the seed (faith). The mustard seed is small but powerful. Once the little mustard seed is planted in the ground, it will only create what its DNA has been programmed to produce, that which God designed it to yield—a mustard plant. The mustard seed contains the substance of the thing hoped for—a mustard plant.

This parable reminds us that the world is framed by our faith-filled, spiritual words. Faith-filled words will bring forth the spiritual dimensions that are asked, prayed and hoped for if we will only believe God's Word is true. The Spirit of God is dwelling within us and among us; He is constantly surrounding us. A seed, though small, is *absolute faith* that will generate whatever we say, pray, decree and desire. We must learn how to seed *absolute faith* in order to obtain the creative, miracle-working God kind of faith, where nothing is impossible.

> *The force of faith empowers our desires to change by giving birth to another measure of Christ within us.*

It is the faith of God that makes us God-conscious. It is God consciousness that enlightens us to be what He desires for us to become. It is this God kind of faith that gives us (and seals us in the revelatory vision) the knowledge of who we are in Christ. Having seen our future by the faith of God (and staying focused in the expression of those feelings), we mature into that state of being.

As Believers, we are called to change the world. To be world changers, we must lose ourselves to become the IAM characteristics, attributes and power that reside within the Christ in us. It is Christ who is our hope of obtaining glory. For more on how to become a world changer, you may read my book *So You Want the Change the World? The Power of Expectation* published by DestinyImage.com.

We live in a supernatural time where the invisible things are becoming visible. If we learn how to connect heaven and earth together, nothing shall be impossible for us! Each year the celebration of Passover empowers us to escape death by stepping into a new and higher mansion of God. The whole earth is crying out for the Sons of God to be revealed so that they can manifest the office level of the Seven Spirits of God listed in Isaiah 11:2. All things are impregnated and birthed, then emerge and take form out of our reservoir or measure of faith in God. *According to your faith let it be done to you* (Matthew 9:29).

After ideas and beliefs are formed, from out of the faith of God, the imagination will cause them to grow out of their infant (seed) stages. Beliefs grow into their full maturity (as a Tree of Life), in order to reach their potential, by bearing spiritual fruit twelve months out of the year.

> *In the middle of its street, and on either side of the river, was the Tree of Life, which bore twelve fruits, each tree yielding its fruit every month. The leaves of the tree were for the healing of the nations* (Revelation 22:2).

To receive an answer to prayer, a healing or a miracle cure, *My soul waits silently for God alone, for my expectation is from Him alone* (Psalm 62:5).

For the earnest expectation of the creation eagerly waits for the revealing of the Sons of God (Romans 8:19).

The Sons of God, who manifest the formidable power of God as One New Man, must be confident of their faith being in God alone in order to cure a terminal disease in themselves or in others.

> *Then shall your light break forth like the morning, and your healing your restoration and the power of a new life shall spring forth speedily; your righteousness your rightness, your justice, and your right relationship with God shall go before you conducting you to peace and prosperity, and the glory of the Lord shall be your rear guard* (Isaiah 58:8).

The failure to manifest a healing or to receive an instant, miraculous cure is usually because of some false idea or misunderstanding that is due to the erroneous teaching of man's traditions, doubt or unbelief. Sometimes it is because the person has placed his or her faith in medicine or medical professionals alone instead of trusting in God and

> Focused faith empowers us to join with and manifest the things we desire or hope for, giving the invisible spiritual truths a grand entrance into our visible material life.

the healing, life-giving power of His Word.

If someone is in pain, it is very difficult for him or her to deny what his or her physical senses are screaming. It is much easier for the infirmed person to go by his or her natural emotions or feelings, the facts of the intellect. It is easy to doubt the truth of God's Word. For us to transform a present physical condition of infirmity into one of being healed and whole, we must focus the attention of our imagination on the true, authentic, lovely, beautiful, noble, real things that are pure, holy, merciful, kind, honorable, admirable and respectable and of a good report. Always fasten your thoughts on every glorious work of God, praising Him always for He alone is worthy.

> The truth found in the Word of God brings to life and portrays the visions we have seen as facts.

Why would we continue to wait in a weakened condition to be healed? Focusing our imagination on being healed now will instantly bring forth joy unspeakable that is full of glory. Why wait four more months to gather in your harvest of healing when Christ has already paid the price for your health and well-being on the cross thousands of years ago?

Fear produces burnout. It is time to trade in the fevered ashes of sickness and dis-ease for the beauty of God's glorious salvation and miracle-working power. *For He says: "In an acceptable time I have heard you, and in the day of salvation I have helped you." Behold, now is the accepted time; behold, now is the day of salvation* (2 Corinthians 6:2).

Once we understand the meanings of God's spiritual and symbolic picture language and actualize the symbols that the Spirit has shown us, they become a real working part of us. Spiritual knowledge empowers us to build upon a broad and an unshakeable biblical foundation. The truth found in the Word of God brings to life and portrays the visions we have seen as facts. *But when the Helper comes, whom I shall send to you from the Father, the Spirit of Truth who proceeds from the Father, He will testify of Me* (John 15:26).

In Scripture, we see a lot of dual components that produce faith when the two concepts are linked, connected or we join them together to form the power of agreement. *Can two walk together, unless they are agreed* (Amos

3:3)?

When we discipline both our conscious and subconscious, along with our soul and spirit, we empower them to unite and agree to walk together in one body, with each flowing in one accord. They learn to function together as one entity that can walk in a unified front. This single mind can align with the Holy Spirit's superior power and the mind of Christ.

When our mind is singularly focused on pleasing God, we are given a visual blueprint. God outlines and designs a plan that both shows and tells us how to accomplish all that God has set forth within us to do. The perfect man exercises a conscious discipline in every area of his life (spirit, soul and body). *But I discipline my body and bring it into subjection, lest, when I have preached to others, I myself should become disqualified* (1 Corinthians 9:27). When people are at peace with themselves, having resolved their own personal internal and external conflicts, it is easier to walk in unity with another.

Husbands and wives that pray together stay together in the oneness of wedded bliss. Husbands are commanded by God to love their wives. God directs wives to honor and respect their husbands. Their unified, mutual agreement on spiritual beliefs or a common purpose or plan empowers the couple to maintain a powerful spiritual and physical bond in a harmonious marriage. Consistent times of prayer and wise, godly counsel produces synchronization that cuts down on the risks of a couple separating or divorcing.

Honest, open transparency eliminates problems and uncovers any hidden, false, toxic political agendas (by sincerely resolving opposing opinions and being gracious, kind and truthful with each other) before the marriage covenant or business contract takes place. Our current reality will transition into a higher place of genuineness when we are inspired to only accept creative ideas that are positive facts or solutions. These facts or solutions are to be developed and acted upon in congruence. Every problem comes with a solution when we seek God's wis-

> *Our current reality will transition into a higher place of genuineness when we are inspired to only accept creative ideas that are positive facts or solutions.*

dom for the answers that reside within our spirit. We should never waste our valuable time considering things that do not enhance, build, produce or increase the measure of peace and happiness in our life.

Let Us Pray

Dear Jesus, show me the superior path, and lead and guide me by the presence of the Holy Spirit. I ask that the Spirit of God will counsel, instruct and teach me how to prosper on the path of justice, knowledge and understanding. Conform me into your image so that I can follow after Your ways. Fill the imagination of my heart with your eternal love. Help me to build a firm, fruitful foundation on Your living Word so that I can understand the deep and secret mysteries found within Your heart. Cleanse me of any limiting beliefs so that I can obtain another measure of Christ deep within my soul. Deliver me from all fear, sickness and disease.

Lord, enable my faith to connect me to the creative life force in God. Teach me how to exhibit the God-kind-of faith in order to release a creative motion that manifests answers to my prayers. Help me to focus my absolute faith on obtaining the things I hope for and the spiritual truths materializing in my life. Impart and release Your miracle healing power in me so that I can perform miracles in the mighty name of Jesus. Give me the skill to understand Your spiritual, symbolic picture language. Cause my heart and soul to agree with You and all You do in complete unity so that we can walk together as One New Man. Amen.

CHAPTER TEN

Spiritual Intuition

The Christ that lives within the Believer is the Spirit of God. The Spirit of the Lord knows and perceives all things. God is able to know the imaginative thoughts and hear the unspoken intents of every person's heart.

Have you ever tried to remember someone's name, and no matter how hard you tried it would not come to you? Stop trying, change the subject and try to relax, for this and every type of intuition comes like a thief in the night when you least expect. Spiritual intuition does not require previous knowledge or education. Spiritual intuition is being taught from within by the Holy Spirit. The answer to our question or problem just comes to us through the King of King's intuition, just like a light bulb that just pops on unannounced. After the Spirit reveals the solution, we need to engage our intellectual reasoning from the renewed mind of Christ in order to accurately complete any new task.

Jesus is the Living Word of God. He is eternally alive, sharp and a quick discerner of the thoughts and goals of the imagination and aims of the heart. God has ways of doing things that are beyond our reasoning capabilities, yet He never fails. When we pray for guidance, we can cast all of our cares upon the Lord, for He cares for us.

Intuition comes through slight impressions, feelings, creative ideas, yet, at times, we are too uptight or fearful to recognize them. Tense or apprehensive fear or a depressed or despondent mood of bitterness makes receiving spiritual intuition impossible. The Bible teaches that words of revelation are heard from inside as a thought, imagination or a still voice that is alive, astute, perceptive and discerning. *In the beginning was the Eternal Word, and the Word was with God, and the Word was God* (John 1:1).

Words contain a creative power that can produce life or death, health or disease, unity or division, harmony or discord, wealth or poverty. Positive words frame and create states, and they build worlds. Happy, joy-filled moods strengthen us, while negative, hate-filled words tear down people, terminate relationships and destroy homes by constructing division that separates by driving in wedges.

> *God has ways of doing things that are beyond our reasoning capabilities, yet He never fails..*

> *For the Word of God is living and powerful, and sharper than any two-edged sword, piercing even to the division of soul and spirit, and of joints and marrow, and is a discerner of the thoughts and intents of the heart or imagination* (Hebrews 4:12).

The Bible explains that it is within the heart of a person that their thoughts, lack of character and belief systems are first formed, then acted upon. *For out of the 'unregenerate' heart proceed evil thoughts, murders, adulteries, fornications, and thefts, false witness, and blasphemies* (Matthew 15:19).

The Bible teaches the Believer to cast down and hold captive every evil, sinful, opposing, doubt-filled thought that is contrary to the loving nature and ingenious power of God. *Casting down arguments and every high thing that exalts itself against the knowledge of God, bringing every thought into captivity to the obedience of Christ* (2 Corinthians 10:5). However, due to our religious upbringings or limited understanding of the ways of God, we often hold our life-giving imagination captive.

When we do not use our imagination correctly to house God's inspired thoughts, we clip the wings of our creative expressions; they are not able to get off the ground to soar. We desire to prosper but cannot see how to accomplish our destiny when we hold our innovative imagination captive in a cage that is surrounded by fear and guarded by legalistic traditions that promote doubt and unbelief.

Imagine whatever you want, and decide it's possible. Then spread your wings, and the breath of the Spirit will carry you up and beyond all limitations. When others say, "It cannot be done!", escape the familiar, and do it anyway.

Businesspeople need to develop spiritual intuition to succeed. As entrepreneurs, we must learn to recognize and heed the subjective, spontaneous voice of wisdom so that God's intuition can guide us to triumph in all of our ways, thoughts and deeds. The entrepreneur always seeks for transformation, answers to its call and utilizes the needed change as an opportunity to develop, knowing that in the middle of every challenge lies a new prospect for success.

Entrepreneurs see little difference between obstacles and opportunity, because they adjust to every situation to turn both to their advantage.

The Holy Spirit can read our minds. He knew our every thought and desire before we were even conceived. The holy angels of God are able to discern our thoughts in prayer, dreams and visions. They come to answer the requests of our heart before we awake to verbalize or make known our desires.

> *But while Joseph thought* (imagined) *about these things, behold, an angel of the Lord appeared to him in a dream, saying, "Joseph, son of David, do not be afraid to take Mary your wife, for that which is conceived in her is of the Holy Spirit"* (Matthew 1:20).

Jesus was able to hear the thoughts of people that were not verbalized with words but only expressed within the privacy of their own mind. *But Jesus knew their thoughts* (imaginations), *and said to them: "Every kingdom divided against itself is brought to desolation, and every city or house divided against itself will not stand"* (Matthew 12:25). Believers are of the Kingdom of Light; we are known as the Body, House or Temple of God. We are to live by faith, not by fear.

> Intuition comes through slight impressions, feelings or creative ideas, yet at times we are too uptight or fearful to recognize them.

Jesus discerned the religious leader's jealous hatred, legalistic rage and violent desire toward Him, even though it was still safely contained and stewing within the four walls of their stony hearts.

> *But He* (Jesus) *knew their thoughts, and said to the man who had the withered hand, "Arise and stand here." And he arose and stood. Then Jesus said to them, "I will ask you one thing: Is it lawful on the Sabbath to do good or to do evil, to save life or to destroy?" And when He had looked around at them all, He said to the man, "Stretch out your hand." And he did so, and his hand was restored as whole as the other. But they were filled with rage, and discussed with one another what they might do to Jesus* (Luke 6:8–11).

Jesus was able to be consciously aware of living in a bilocated, heavenly place while still living upon the earth. Jesus could see, hear and observe what was going on in heaven. At the same time, He was compassionately ministering to the hurt, withered, diseased and lame people on earth. *Then Jesus answered and said to them, "Most assuredly, I say to you, the Son can do nothing of Himself, but what He sees the Father do; for whatever He does, the Son also does in like manner"* (John 5:19).

Jesus could look into people's souls to determine the root causes of their sickness or disease. He knew if they had been born deformed in order for their creative or recreative miracle to give God the glory. He knew if the sickness, disease or iniquity was due to a personal issue or generational sins that released a curse to the fourth family line of ancestors. Jesus knew if their infirmity was the result of demonic spirits that inhabited their body. The bookstore at DreamsDecoder.com offers a Healing Card that determines the root causes of sickness and disease.

> *The power of spiritual agreement is able to relocate the answers to our prophetic prayers, bringing them out of their waiting chambers in heavenly places in order to give them expression in the reality of our present conditions.*

The physical realm was not a limitation for Jesus. He knew how to look beyond the natural to see and perceive God moving in the divine, supernatural realm of the Spirit. Jesus could see the spirit that rested on individuals or motivated people from within. Jesus could also see the manifestation of the Spirit of Faith in and on those who believed in Him. Jesus knew when people had faith and trusted in His healing, miracle-working power, and He could also see the evil spirits that lurked in the souls of man. He easily discerned their thoughts and wicked intentions. All of their hidden plotting and foul schemes were laid open and bared before Jesus.

> *So He* (Jesus) *got into a boat, crossed over, and came to His own city. Then behold, they brought to Him a paralytic lying on a bed. When Jesus saw their faith, He said to the paralytic, "Son, be of good cheer; your sins are forgiven you." And at once some of the scribes said within them, "This Man blasphemes!" But Jesus, knowing their thoughts, said, "Why do you think* (imagine) *evil in your hearts? For which is easier, to say, 'Your sins are forgiven you' or to say 'Arise and walk?' But that you may know that the Son of Man has power on earth to forgive sins"—then He said to the paralytic, "Arise, take up your bed, and go to your house." And he arose and departed to his house. Now when the multitudes saw it, they marveled and glorified God, who had given such power to men* (Matthew 9:1–8).

Faith is a propelling force that causes matter, entities and events to transfer, realign or rearrange. Faith repositions people so that they can move into a new location or realm, or so that they can advance into a larger sphere of influence in order to take advantage of a phenomenal opportunity or to possess a presently manifested mansion. The power of spiritual agreement is able to relocate the answers to our prophetic prayers, bringing them out of their waiting chambers in heavenly places in order to give them expression in the reality of our present conditions. *And now I have told you before it comes, that when it does come to pass, you may believe* (John 14:26).

Let Us Pray

Dear Lord Jesus, search and know my heart, and discern the thoughts and intents of my heart. Cleanse my heart of all lack, disbelief, evil thoughts of hatred, false witness, blasphemies, murder, adulteries, fornication and theft. Bring my imaginations into the captivity and obedience of Christ. Help me to look beyond the natural to see and perceive God moving in the supernatural realm. Open my eyes to see the Holy Spirit resting on people for healing, salvation or miracles. Let me accurately discern the needs of their hearts. Let me pray and prophesy heavenly things that are waiting to give their expressions here on earth. Amen.

CHAPTER ELEVEN

Creative Power

God completed all of creation, the animals, fish, birds, plant, oceans, sky, space and all of the vast innumerable heavens and the earth, in just six days. We know this because it is recorded in the Bible in the first book of Genesis. So it is fact that all we want, need or desire was previously created, it is already available and waiting for us in the glory realms. God made everything beautiful in its perfect time. Then on the seventh day, God entered into rest. *Six days you shall do your work, but the seventh day you shall rest and keep Sabbath, that your ox and your donkey may rest, and the son of your bondwoman, and the alien, may be refreshed* (Exodus 23:12).

Whatever God says, does or creates remains forever. Man should fear God with great reverence; for nothing can be added to His creation, and nothing can be taken from it. Whatever was is already. Whatever will be is now. That's how it has always been, and that's how it will always be with God. That which is present has previously been. What is to be in the future has existed before.

> *That which has been is what will be, that which is done is what will be done, and there is nothing new under the sun. Is there anything of which it may be said, "See, this is new"? It has already been in ancient times before us. There is no remembrance of former things, nor will there be any remembrance of things that are to come by those who will come after* (Ecclesi-

astes 1:9–11).

God resurrects that which has disappeared into the distant past, to bring vision forth so that an image can be seen and recycled and can pass before us again. God's will shall be established in us, and the will of His Spirit will also be reestablished in us in time. God requires us to give an account of what has passed, while inviting us to press into Him in order to obtain the unseen future (see Ecclesiastes 3).

To access the realms of heaven or the Kingdom of God that is within us, all we have to do is seek to intimately know the person of Jesus Christ. When we seek His face, knock on the door of His heart and ask Him to awaken, resurrect or come up within us, our imagination is illuminated as Christ reveals more of Himself to us. When we hear or see the door of Jesus' heart open, we can enter into the spirit. For everyone who asks, receives. He who seeks God first with all of his heart will find Him. To him who knocks, it will be opened to you.

> *God resurrects that which has disappeared into the distant past to bring vision forth so that an image can be seen and recycled and can pass before us again.*

The imagination is the key that unlocks what shall be when we believe and see our desires fulfilled. Every possibility already exists, but we need to open the eyes of our imagination to see what the world should be, and then we need to open our mouth to decree it is done.

To discover something new, allow your imagination to escape the realm of predictability by creating a different door. Keep knocking at wisdom's door until she opens her abundant storehouse of vast opportunities for you to enter in and prosper as never before.

The imagination opens the door to the inevitable, foreseeable future so that we are no longer locked into the predictable certainty of a mundane existence. Prayer brings yesterday's imaginations into today's triumphant victories of reality. Our imagination scouts ahead of us to align us with future opportunities so that we are prepared to make those images into today's realities.

The Virgin Mary

We learned about the awakened imagination, imaginative desire and creative power in previous volumes. Dreaming with an awakened imagination empowers us to imagine greatness when we cannot see it in ourselves and to achieve the impossible when we do not think we can. Dreams show us how to become all we ever imagined.

The following biblical accounts illustrate God's imaginative, creative power that resides within our sanctified imagination. This creative, imaginative power allows us to align with His plans and purposes as we seek to operate as true Sons of God.

Jesus comes knocking on the door of every person's imaginative heart to impregnate us with desire, just as the angel Gabriel came to the Virgin Mary and asked if she would submit to the will of God's creative presence within her womb. Mary's response was, *Behold the maidservant of the Lord! Let it be to me according to your word* (Luke 1:38). The imagination is the womb that conceives a word of truth, an idea, seed, thought or prophecy. The new wine womb stretches and continues to grow until it gives birth to the full evidence of things hoped for by manifesting them in the future.

The Virgin Mary was a virtuous, young lady who had not yet married her fiancé, Joseph. She had no natural husband to make her womb fruitful, yet she conceived the Savior of the World by the Holy Spirit. *For your Maker is your husband, the Lord of hosts is His name; and your Redeemer is the Holy One of Israel; He is called the God of the whole earth* (Isaiah 54:5).

> As we grow in the understanding of how to manifest the Holy Spirit's presence, ways and truth, another dimension of power, characteristic or attribute of God is able to emerge within our being.

Agreeing with God's life-giving, creative will redeems us from a fallen, barren state of death. The name Mary means *water that flows with the ability to move, fill in and take on the shape of anything into which it is poured*. Mary was willing and obedient; she was pliable in the hand of God.

When we, like Mary, embrace the Holy Spirit's knocking at the door of our heart, we open up our imagination to see His will and receive His invitation to conceive. Once revelation impregnates us with purposes, we are able to carry full-term the seeds of a divinely inspired idea we have been given. We birth the Christ child within. As He grows and matures within us, we will continually manifest the creative Kingdom of God and express all that heaven contains.

A microscopic fragment of God's light entered our being at conception. At salvation, His Spirit came in at His fullness. Yet we do not recognize the magnitude of His grandeur all at once. Our ability to recognize the presence of Christ awakening within us is a gradual process. It is not until we are born again that we can even begin to conceive of the measures of His greatness.

> By surrendering to the preparation of the Holy Spirit and agreeing with God's plans for our lives, we become equal partners and joint heirs with Christ.

Before the imagination is awakened to live in Christ, it functions at a carnal, earthly, destructive level that produces pain, wounding, suffering and evil, lustful thoughts that lead to death or murder. *Therefore, the Jews sought all the more to kill Him, because He not only broke the Sabbath, but also said that God was His Father, making Himself equal with God* (John 5:18).

When we take on God's image, we take on His loving, divine nature. The character of God dwelling within us causes us to increase in the measure of revelation knowledge, compassion and power that is demonstrated in and through our life. *Who, being in the form of God, did not consider it robbery to be equal with God* (Philippians 2:6).

As we grow in the understanding of how to manifest the Holy Spirit's presence, ways and truth, another dimension of power, characteristic or attribute of God is able to emerge within our being. God expands His Kingdom within our hearts by revealing more and more of His eternal essence and plans to our imaginations. *You did not choose Me, but I chose you and appointed you that you should go and bear fruit, and that your fruit should remain, so that whatever you ask the Father in My name He may give you* (John 15:16).

The Virgin Mother of Jesus is the most famous virgin in the world. She was chosen by God to bear His Son, Jesus Christ. The fruit of her womb is still bearing eternal fruit today.

The Ten Virgins

The Bible also compares ten virgins (see Matthew 25:1–13).

> Five virgins were wise, and five virgins were foolish. The five wise virgins were practical and well-prepared for the future. They had joined with, became and related to the truths of God. They knew and understood that it was the anointing that broke the yokes. The oil of God's presence burning in their heart kept them flexible, moving forward in their desire for intimacy. It was the result of wisdom that they carried an extra flask of oil with them to keep their revelatory lamps in the window of their soul burning. The fragrant, anointing oil they smeared on themselves was a sweet, aromatic incense that drew their lover to them. The oil of His presence molded them into the image and likeness of the Bridegroom.
>
> The wise virgins were alert, awake and prepared. They were willing to take all the time that was needed to wait upon the manifestation of the Bridegroom and His Bride's coming. The wise virgins had developed a personal, intimate relationship with the Bridegroom. They had helped to prepare the Bride, although the Bride had decked herself with garland and adorned herself with jewels to make herself ready (see Isaiah 61:10; Revelation 19:7).
>
> The Bridegroom didn't come when the virgins expected, all ten of them grew drowsy and fell asleep (see Mark 13:35–37). Then suddenly, in the middle of the night, they were all awakened by a shout, "Get up! The Bridegroom is here! Come out and have an encounter with Him" (see 1 Thessalonians 5:2)!
>
> Quickly, all of the virgins got up and trimmed their lamps with the fire of the Spirit. But the foolish virgins who had

not applied the truth of God to their lives were not flexible (moving in an old, dry wineskin), prepared or ready. They were running on spiritual vapors, for their oil was running out. They rushed to the five wise virgins and begged, "Please, share your oil (joy, anointing, revelation) with us, because our lamps are going out!"

"No! We can't," they replied. "We don't have enough for all of us. You'll have to go and buy some oil for yourselves!" While the five unprepared, foolish virgins were out buying oil, the Bridegroom appeared (the number five means *redemptive life, atoning actions, in favor and grace of the five-fold ministry*).

The five wise virgins who were prepared (ready in season and out of season, waiting on Christ's appearing) were escorted inside with the Bridegroom. The few virgins who were prepared and full of wisdom joined the wedding party to enjoy the feast. The door was locked behind the five wise virgins and the Bridegroom's friends, family and guests.

Later, the five foolish virgins came running up to knock on the door. But it was too late. The Bridegroom did not open the door to the unwise virgins, even though they urgently pleaded, "Lord, Lord, let us come in!"

Instead, He called back, "Go away! Do I even know any of you? No! I can assure you that I don't know you at all! My presence is not within any of you, nor is My fragrant essence upon your presence. None of you look, smell, sound, act or move like Me." These five foolish virgins were trying to arrive at an expected end without going through the anointed transformation process. They could not gain entrance through the only door to the Father: Jesus.

This powerful parable tells us that we should stay awake, be alert and keep developing an intimate, current relationship with Jesus. No one knows the day or hour when the Bridegroom will appear, except His Father. No one knows the Son, except the Father. No one knows the Father, except the Son. Jesus Christ chooses the people to whom He will reveal the Father.

Manifesting the power of God's love that dwells within us brings forth eternal fruit that remains. We experience God in His fullness when we recognize the universal expanse of His ever-increasing presence that is living within us. By surrendering to the preparation of the Holy Spirit and agreeing with God's plans for our lives, we become equal partners and joint heirs with Christ.

Because God's words of faith are intermingled in the core vision of our heart's imagination, we can manifest His unlimited power.

> *But the righteousness of faith speaks in this way, "Do not say in your heart, 'Who will ascend into heaven?'* (that is, to bring Christ down from above) *or 'Who will descend into the abyss?'"* (that is, to bring Christ up from the dead) *But what does it say? "The Word is near you; it is in your mouth and in your* (imagination) *heart* (the word of faith which we preach)*: that if you confess with your mouth the Lord Jesus and believe in your heart that God has raised Him from the dead, you will be saved. For with the heart one believes unto righteousness, and with the mouth confession is made unto salvation"* (Romans 10:6–10).

We yield our bodies to give free expression to God's powerful ways when we step out of the narrow confines of a culture's boat to walk on the water with Christ. We advance by revoking the regulatory traditions of man's religious trappings so that we can walk on the buoyant, sustaining waters by placing our faith in God. All Things are possible to those who believe that the desires of our heart carry the blessings of God's imaginative, creative power.

Let Us Pray

You are the great Eternal One, the maker of heaven and earth. You are the One who formed me in my mother's womb. You knew me before I was born. All of my days have been numbered and seen by You before I came into earthly existence. Thank You, Lord Jesus, that Your Word states that the good work You have begun in me, You will also bring to a completion.

My desire is to be transformed into Your image and likeness so that I may dwell with You forever in eternity. Help me to imagine and see everything You have designed for me to be and do. Assist me in keeping an accurate account of all the things You have done for me in the past, so I can celebrate Your great name. Teach me how to press into You so that I can obtain the unseen future. I want to know You intimately in spirit and in truth.

IAM asking, seeking and knocking on the door of Your heart with all my might and strength of imagination. Awaken within me the imagination and creative powers so that I can activate the measure of faith You have given me to align and achieve Your plans and the purposes You have ordained me to walk in as a Son of God. Help me to grow and function in a greater measure of revelation knowledge, compassion and demonstrative power. Allow Your Kingdom to continue to expand within me as I learn to embrace more of Your eternal essence. I want to be like one of the wise virgins. Show me how to be awake, alert, practical, practiced, planned and prepared for the future. Fill me with the oil of Your presence so that my heart continually burns with a passionate, intimate love for You alone. Amen.

CHAPTER TWELVE

Connection—The Law of Attraction

Have an open mind to learn about everything godly that is spiritually true, for revelation knowledge will help you to rightly discern God's truth. Be eager to explore the possibilities and relationships that present themselves. But do not focus your time or spend your energy or efforts on attracting temporal, earthly, material things. We receive that which we desire by consciously assuming the actions of the new person that we desire to be in Christ. We become different yet better when we rearrange our thoughts and ideas by receiving the concepts that we have envisioned.

When we adopt a new, God-given outlook on life, we awaken as if we are already a new creation who has become that wholesome person of influence. We cannot attract things to us by exercising a physical force or violence toward someone or something. As our spirit focuses on loving God, by seeking His presence first and foremost, all these other earthly things will be added to us.

God is the master Creator! Unlike God, we do not have the ability to create something from nothing, but we can determine what part of His creation we will enjoy and steward. No one possesses enough knowledge about the process of how things come into being to warrant being a negative pessimist. Progress is impossible if you always do things the same way that you have always done them.

Repent and change your mind in order to find success in your life as every new day dawns. Be free to be your best self, and think on the higher thoughts that God has toward you. Enjoy your own individual taste, and express your unique desires as God has called you to do. State with confidence, "My mind is open to new, creative ideas. It is flexible and curious. It is able to learn whatever I need in order to advance and succeed. My mind is active and brilliant; it is not ridged, tired or restricted."

Remember, we cannot give away or share what we do not have. No one can impart to others what they do not already know, have experienced or currently possess. However, we can recognize, awaken or resurrect what is already within them. We will never be convinced of a truth that we do not personally believe, no matter how powerful that truth is. We accelerate and prosper when we agree with the vision that God has placed in our imaginative heart. Seeing what God wants to do and yielding our body as a vessel for His power, anointing or glory to flow through causes us to become a conduit that channels God's internal, resting presence. It releases His Spirit to flow and manifest to the outside world.

> *When we adopt a new, God-given outlook on life, we awaken as if we are already a new creation who has become that wholesome person of influence.*

Visionary dreams from God come to accelerate changes in us that have the power to initiate revolutionary transformation in us and in others. From the moment the dream is fashioned within our mind's eye, God begins to relate to us differently—as if we have already matured into that new person. God shows us who we really are as we begin to walk with Him in a higher dimension. God continues to interact with us as if we have already been physically changed into the different man or woman that He destined for us to be in the future because we have, at present, been changed in the Spirit.

In the realm of the Spirit, what has been seen in vision form in the imagination is a now reality, a memory of an already happened event. The visions of the imagination are a transformational catalyst. The visions of our mind's eye empower us to become a better, brand new and different person. Through vision, we see ourself differently. We treat ourself today as if we are already who we are designed to be in the future by doing what we were created to do.

When a vision manifests in your spirit, it is important to embrace, mimic and demonstrate the changes that are seen. Agree with God's higher plans and broader purposes. Then begin to act like what you saw. Begin doing the things that you have been shown. Possess the power to manifest this new identity by believing in you. If you lack a certain characteristic, trait or attribute, assume that you already have it. Treat yourself as if you are already what you are to become in the future. If you have seen yourself being taught to do something new and felt yourself doing that act in the Spirit realm, you can now manifest that same act in the natural, earthly realm of existence.

Our thoughts become words. Our words become the actions that attract to us what we thought yesterday, think today, believe, speak and act upon. We reap what we sow, earning in proportion to what we give out. We call forth into the present world environment of our personal being what we currently know, believe as truth and consistently practice. We attract more of what we ask for, have already seen, believed, dished out to or sown toward others.

Wisdom always avoids all forms of fear. Wisdom will elude stress and physical, emotional and especially spiritual weaknesses. Wisdom allows us to avoid all forms of negativity, guilt and shame. It is vital that we intentionally change our thoughts to reflect God's higher, pure thoughts of love. By increasing the frequency levels of our thought patterns, we are able to embrace God's life-giving, creative ways as a life-giving spirit. Never settle or agree with being less when more is always available in God. Abundance is always available! So why settle for poverty and lack?

> *From the moment the dream is fashioned within our mind's eye, God begins to relate to us differently—as if we have already matured into that new person.*

We determine if our degree of blessing will increase or multiply according to the measure of faith that we possess in the belief that God is good. We need to know that God has already abundantly blessed us with every good gift from before the foundations of the world. If God has already supplied everything we need, He will continue to bless us as we grow in our ability to apprehend His blessings and higher spiritual ways. Imagine with all your heart, dream with all your mind and achieve with every gift you have been given.

Prosperity is bestowed upon us when we possess a strong desire to give all of our strength to loving God. By learning to love God, we learn to love ourself and our enemies, and we learn how to serve others.

Personal Refection Moment

1. How much love, joy, peace, gentleness, kindness and long-suffering do you possess?
2. How much are you able to give to or sow into others?

To know God, our spirit has to learn how to rest and meditate in the beautiful substance of His presence. When we prayerfully embrace the quiet silence of our soul, we are then able to hear and echo the Spirit's peaceful words of wisdom that ring true with every beat of our heart.

We all dance to a specific, syncopated beat or melodious tune. We each sing to the internal music that we hear deep within the rhythmic pounding of our own heart. Listening with our spirit allows us to hear the thunderous sounds of heaven. When we align our spirit with heaven, even the very blood coursing through our veins moves in perfect harmony with the choirs of winged angels, cherubim and seraphim.

> *In the realm of the Spirit, what has been seen in vision form in the imagination is a now reality, a memory of an already happened event.*

Our attitudes, thoughts and beliefs determine our current life conditions as well as the quality of life that we will acquire in the future.

Mature Believers have trained their spiritual eyes to see faith when the Spirit of Truth is resting on them and shining on others. Ask God to open your spiritual eyes so that you can SEE! God the Father, Jesus the Son and the Holy Spirit are a tripartite Spirit person. We are too mature in our whole person, body, soul and spirit. The natural, unregenerated man cannot know, understand or see the things of the Spirit. The eyes of your heart are the eyes of the Spirit.

> *Therefore I also, after I heard of your faith in the Lord Jesus and your love for all the saints, do not cease to give thanks* (causes multiplication) *for you, making mention of you in my prayers: that the God of our Lord Jesus Christ, the Father of glory, may give to you the spirit of wisdom and revelation in the knowledge of Him, the eyes of your understanding* (means going into the future) *being enlightened; that you may know what is the hope of His calling, what are the riches of the glory of His inheritance in the saints, and what is the exceeding greatness of His power toward us who believe, according to the working of His mighty power* (resurrection), *which He worked in Christ when He raised Him from the dead and seated Him at His right hand in the heavenly places,* (mansions) *far above all principality and power and might and dominion, and every name that is named, not only in this age but also in that which is to come. And He put All Things under His feet, and gave Him to be head over All Things to the Church, which is His body, the fullness of Him who fills all in all* (Ephesians 1:15–23).

Fellowship with Jesus requires us to develop the ability to see, hear and be led by the three-in-one Godhead. The Holy Spirit teaches us to pray to and worship God and to move in spirit and in truth (see John 4:24). *And do not be conformed to this world, but be transformed by the renewing of your mind, that you may prove what is that good and acceptable and perfect will of God* (Romans 12:2). That which God has begun in us He is always faithful to complete!

> *I was in the Spirit on the Lord's Day* (to see visions), *and I heard* (God's voice) *behind me a loud voice, as of a trumpet, saying, "I am the Alpha* (beginning) *and the Omega* (end), *the First and the Last," and, "What you see, write in a book"* (Revelation 1:10–11).

When we are consciously awareness of the Kingdom of God living within us, we walk and dwell in the Spirit. *For in Him we live and move and have our being in the Spirit* (Acts 17:28). The vast limitlessness of God's Kingdom is not of this world, but it dwells within the heart of earth-dwelling man.

> *As a man thinks of himself,* (calculating, processing and reasoning in his thoughts to develop concepts, opinions and considerations) *imagines* (develops creative possibilities, ideas, answers and solutions) *in his heart, so is he* (Proverb 23:27).

Are you a grasshopper, or are you a giant slayer? Are you a caterpillar, or are you a beautiful butterfly?

To be successful we need to think in reasonable thoughts, to develop logical, commonsense conceptions while joining the aspect of dreaming imaginative, creative possibilities. Our thoughts determine our tomorrows and distant future. Because our constant thoughts produce choices, values, principles and actions, it is not our desires that actually define who we really are.

If you do not like your current results or life situations, determine to take responsibility for the materials you hear and review. Use God as your primary source of vision. Exercise self-control to selectively filter the programming you are feeding your mind to change your thoughts, actions, habits, character and destiny. Remember the old saying, "You are what you eat!" Spend time developing a sound Christlike mind, then align the strength of your physical body to carry out your moral convictions.

> *I will set no sinful or wicked thing before my eyes. I refuse to gaze on that which is sordid or vulgar things. I despise works of evil people. I detest the worthless deeds of those who stray, fall away and anything that moves my heart away from you. Evil will not get a hold on me. I will not let evil hold me in its grip* (Psalm 101:3).

Believers with clean hands and a clear Christ consciousness, those who are pure in heart (imagination), will SEE God. What you continually think on and see yourself doing in the realm of the Spirit will eventually manifest in the natural world. If I think God's thoughts toward me and believe that I can do All Things He has planned for me to accomplish through Christ who strengthens me, the things I imagine myself doing will become a manifested reality.

Focused, faith-filled thoughts empower us to manifest the Kingdom of

God and His righteousness. We are to behold and mirror God in the Spirit.

> *But we all, with unveiled face, beholding as in a mirror the glory of the Lord, are being transformed into that same level or image of glory, from glory to an ever-increasing level of greater glory, just as by the Spirit of the Lord* (2 Corinthians 3:18).

Jesus considered the imagination as a present reality because the imagination is the language of the realm of the Spirit.

> *While we do not look at the things which are seen* (natural, physical realm), *but at the things which are not seen* (the invisible realm of the Spirit). *For the things which are seen are temporary, but the things which are not seen are eternal* (2 Corinthians 4:18).

Upon what you focus your imagination (whether it is of a positive or negative nature, or whether it is from the Kingdom of Light or from evil that is lurking in the domain of darkness), your power of inventions will bring you into a spiritual connection. *But I say to you that whoever looks at a woman to lust for her has already imagined committing adultery with her in his* (imagination) *heart* (Matthew 5:28).

If you focus upon knowing and experiencing Jesus with the loving emotions of the heart, the creative abilities of the imaginative mind and strength, you will be able to see Him, be like Him and manifest His presence. Jesus said to him, *You shall love the Lord your God with all your heart* (imagination) *with all your soul, and with all your mind* (dionoia, imagination) (Matthew 22:37).

> *If then you were raised with Christ, seek those things which are above, where Christ is, sitting at the right hand of God. Set your mind* (imagination) *on things above, not on things on the earth.*

Set and exercise the mind with the feeling of peaceful, expectant emotions. Reign in the mind with a loving focus. To fence thoughts in, place your imagination and affections on Jesus and All Things above. *For you died, and your life is hidden with Christ in God. When Christ who is our life appears, then you also will appear with Him in glory* (Colossian 3:1–4).

The emotions of love are extremely important in connecting with the Kingdom of God, because God is love!

> *The eyes* (vision or spiritual sight) *of your understanding* (imagination, the inward eyes of your heart) *being enlightened* (to see photographs, images or pictures)*; that you may know* (see and experience) *what is the hope of His calling, what are the riches of the glory of His inheritance in the saints, and what is the exceeding greatness of His power toward us who believe, according to the working of His mighty power* (Ephesians 1:18–19).

The power of hope being placed in the belief of God's greatness empowers us to know how many assets God has given to us. Therefore, we can change to achieve our purpose and destiny in life. We always start to receive revelation of who we are by entering into the outer courts of God's presence in the natural, physical, soul realm. Then, as we enter into prayer, praise and worship, we advance into the door Jesus Christ, becoming conscious of His abiding presence in order to gain entrance into the spiritual realm. There we pause to see and conceive vision, then we agree with God and travail through prayer for a season of time until we can give birth to the fullness of God's plans and purposes,

> *Mature Believers have trained their spiritual eyes to see faith when the Spirit of Truth is resting on them and shining on others.*

> *It is sown a natural body; it is raised a spiritual body. There is a natural body, and there is a spiritual body. And so, it is written, "The first man Adam became a living being." The last Adam became a life-giving spirit. However, the spiritual is not first, but the natural, and afterward the spiritual* (1 Corinthians 15:44–46).

You are a Believer if you believe Jesus is the Word of God with all your heart. You are a Believer if you believe that nothing that you can imagine is impossible for you. Wonderful things happen for those who spend time imagining how to do the impossible. Without the imagination nothing happens.

In Genesis 11:1, the people spoke one language and had unified around one vision. The Bible states that nothing can be restrained from them for which they have imagined. For us to fellowship with Jesus, it requires that we go where He is. Jesus has gone before us into a higher place where He is dwelling with His heavenly Father in mansions of glory.

The thoughts of our mind must move into a visionary state or mansion to see what Jesus is doing. We must focus our imagination on loving Jesus in order to stay at a higher realm of the Spirit. Also, in order to apprehend wisdom to solve problems, to gain an anointing, a healing or a miracle or to sustain our vision in the creative realms of glory, we must focus our imagination on Jesus.

Because God's Kingdom is housed within our earthen bodies, we must ascend into a higher spiritual plain of internal existence. Adam was physically formed from the dust of the earth. For Adam to become a life-giving spirit, God had to breathe the Ruach (life-giving, creative) breath into his being.

Although God's presence and love is constant, our ability to stay focused upon Jesus fluctuates. We must ascend into love and rest there in peace in order to enter into God's realm to worship Him in spirit and truth. In this place of reverence, we gain the revelation knowledge that is needed to continually walk in the light of His Spirit. We know each other by the spirit and by the fruits we produce. The blood of Jesus cleanses us from all sin.

> *Fellowship with Jesus requires us to develop the ability to see, hear and be led by the three-in-one Godhead.*

Faith in God's Word empowers us to move into the spiritual realm to commune with Him. To become conscious of God's eternal presence, we focus on the Kingdom of God by continually hungering and thirsting for His righteousness. To be more effective, we need to intentionally look for and see the angels, cherubim, seraphim and archangels of God. Once we recognize their presence in the atmosphere, we need to incorporate them in our intercession by assigning them tasks and sending them forth to accomplish the Word of God.

The fearful nightmares of the wicked will come upon him, and the desire of the righteous people will be granted (Proverb 10:24).

When our inner faith is quickened from one level of consciousness to another, it continues to rise up from within to exude outside of the body. Man does not lift us into a higher realm of existence; it is the Holy Spirit who teaches us spiritual knowledge. *Delight yourself in doing good deeds and also keep company with the LORD, and He shall give you the best desires* (feelings) *of your heart* (Psalm 37:4).

We are not to hold to any other gods besides Jesus. When we still ourselves, we will know that greater is the God who is in us than he who is in the world.

> *But the anointing which you have received from Him abides in you, and you do not need that anyone teach you; but as the same anointing teaches you concerning All Things, and is true, and is not a lie, and just as it has taught you, you will abide in Him* (1 John 2:27).

Glory often appears as faith manifesting as the Spirit of Truth. *That He would grant you, according to the riches of His glory, to be strengthened with might through His Spirit in the inner man* (Ephesians 3:16). The earth's fullness belongs to the Lord and to all those who dwell in the world.

When Believers exercise the faith of God, they see the light of God shining out of the gates of glory. The head and hands of every Believer contains gates and doors. These spiritual gateways can be lifted up to see God's movements, to hear and feel His comings. These personal gateways of our five senses are opened so that the King of Glory can come flooding in to move into the world through each of our bodies. *"While you have the light, believe in the light, that you may become sons of light." These things Jesus spoke, and departed, and was hidden from them* (John 12:36).

The gift of the Word of Knowledge is a powerful faith building catalyst that immediately manifests the Spirit of Truth.

> *The Lord God has given me the tongue of the learned, that I should know how to speak a word in season to him who is weary. He awakens me morning by morning; He awakens my ear to hear as the learned* (Isaiah 50:4).

The truth of God's Word releases the necessary measure of faith that is sufficient for us to obtain all of our needs, desires or miracles from the realm of glory. The worldly people cannot receive the Spirit of Truth, because they are spiritually blind, not seeing or knowing truth. *The Spirit of Truth, whom the world cannot receive, because it neither sees Him nor knows Him; but you know Him, for He dwells with you and will be in you* (John 14:17).

Opportunities are easily found when we open our eyes to see that doors and gates are within us and surrounding us on every side. *However, when He, the Spirit of truth, has come, He will guide you into all truth; for He will not speak on His own authority, but whatever He hears He will speak; and He will tell you things to come* (John 16:13). But the spiritually blind are unable to receive anything from the Spirit of Truth; their spiritual book is still closed. They are not able to read or understand what has been written for them.

Unbelievers cannot see the spiritual gateways or doors of opportunity. They are not open to diverse inputs or various ideas of others, who could have possibly been friends and assets, simply because they are different. Making many friends in life causes us to advance when we practice the cooperative Golden Rule of harmony—do unto others as you would have them do unto you! Even when truth lovingly provokes the blind unbelievers in a face-to-face confrontation, they do not recognize the person of truth because they have already believed a lie.

The Bible teaches us how to handle conflict when it turns into an aggressive confrontation. *A soft answer turns away wrath* (Proverb 15:1). No one likes to be proven wrong. It is very humbling to be proven wrong, even when we know we have exaggerated the truth. When you are confronted by another, try not to default into an argumentative defense of yourself. Resist retaliating with caustic jabs or by saying unkind things, and don't raise your voice in anger. Learn to manage your response by controlling the tone of your voice. A slow, soft, gentle answer will command more respect than a military tank. With this type of response, the person involved in the discussion will remain more open to considering your point of view and maintaining the conversation.

Good communication skills help to build a profitable relationship where opinions can be shared openly without the fear of a confrontation. Hostile communications may intimidate to win the argument at all cost, but they also waste time and energy. They do not resolve the problem and often permanently destroy relationships. There is no such thing as a good relationship without good open communication.

Respond to conflict in a quiet, peaceable manner. A sweet smile lets people know you are kind, loving and humble. You may not know everything, but you are self-controlled and self-assured that you do have information that will benefit them. Learn to listen to their point of view with an open mind. Look for common ground and things you can agree on. Confirm that you have heard them by stating, "That is an interesting point," or "You know you are probably right!"

> Focused, faith-filled thoughts empower us to manifest the Kingdom of God and His righteousness.

Control your emotions by taking a deep breath before offering an appropriate response. Loud, abrasive, ranting and raving only proves that you are an insecure person. It is always more embarrassing when we find out that we were wrong after we have been screaming our defense at the top of our voices with others in earshot. Downplaying your own knowledge and seeing the value in others and embracing their opinions earns you the right to share your opinion too. It is better to remain open and flexible, getting part of the whole instead of none.

Words are powerful. They determine wartime and peacetime, friends or foes, successes or failures. When conflicts arise learn to be a diplomatic, genuinely, caring person. If you forgive others quickly and never hold a grudge or keep score, you will go far in life.

To know the Spirit of Truth, one must be converted into God's Kingdom of Light and Truth. Believers know truth because they have met and received Christ Jesus. The Spirit of Truth dwells with and lives within the Believer (see John 14:17). The Spirit of Truth comes to lead and guide the Believer into all truth. He does not speak on His own authority, but He shares what He has heard being spoken about the future by the Trinity in heaven (see John16:13).

The Spirit of Truth is part of the heavenly team (Father, Son and Holy

Spirit) that functions as one.

    T – THINK HIGHER THOUGHTS

    E – EXCELLENCE IN EVERY EVENT

    A – ADAPTABLE & ADJUSTABLE

    M – MOTIVATED MOTION

If we disconnect from truth or the realm of faith, we will fail to reach our desired destiny. We are all born to experience certain purposes and accomplish an inevitable destiny that has been reserved just for each one of us. When one purpose is mastered, applied and fulfilled, another emerges from the deep reservoir of possibilities within the individual. Since Believers are eternal beings, we are always evolving, maturing, obtaining, expanding and transforming into the likeness and image of the One who created us, Christ Jesus.

Our thoughts, words and actions create the contents, heights and measure of what we will experience and express in the world. When the mind is content, it is because we are dwelling on thoughts of peace, beauty and happiness. As we continue to focus on being content, we are able to bring that distant vision or desire home to rest within our own heart. The higher our thoughts become, the higher and more noble our ways will become. We manifest miracles and the goodness of God when we learn the ways of God. He is able to cause us to ascend above the natural laws to perform wonders in every area of our life.

Focusing our desire upon knowing the ways of God, by seeking His Kingdom first, empowers us to realize the desires He has hidden in the midst of our heart. Belief in God's unwavering Word solidifies a firm foundation from which we are able to stand to see ourself being transformed into His image and likeness. We are then able to launch into the realm of the Spirit to do the will of the Father, because the imagination is the highest rocket that one can launch.

Fear blocks us from obtaining our desire. Disbelief robs our strength and steals our hopes. In order to prosper, we must believe that what we hope for has already been created and is waiting expectantly on us to ask, seek and knock to acquire it. All we have to do is believe that it is possible to manifest the present reality of the visionary images in our life. By believing we have already received what we see, desire or hope for, we become the new person we have desired to be. Stop allowing the old, perverse, double-minded person of doubt and unbelief to raise its ugly head.

Let Us Pray

Dear Lord Jesus, help me to have an open mind to learn something productive and positive from everyone I meet. I want to rightly discern Your truth. Awaken my imagination so that I can manifest my whole self as a new creation in Christ. Give me the wisdom and ability to seek Your Kingdom first so that all earthly and spiritual things can be added unto me. Help me embrace the positive changes that need to take place in me to become successful in life. I ask that when I awaken, a new day of spiritual enlightenment will have come to me. Renew my brilliant mind by the washing of Your life-giving, creative Word. I come into alignment with Your imaginative heart so that I can see what You have retained for me in the invisible realm of the Spirit.

I long to rest in Your presence. Please impart Your vision to my soul. Help me to discern the spiritual changes that have taken place in me. Make me a better person through dreams and vision. I want to relate to You as a person who has already seen, understood and apprehended their visionary destiny. Empower me to steward what I currently know, but I ask that You continually add to my level of revelation knowledge so that I can gain a greater measure of understanding in order to advance in You. Give me Your wisdom so that I can eliminate all fear, the effects of having a double-mind of doubt and disbelief, emotional stress and physical weaknesses from my life.

Thank You for Your abundant blessings overtaking my life. Train my eyes to see faith resting on others. Awaken my awareness, and remove the veil that covers my face so I can see the ever-present Kingdom of God that resides within me. I long to see God in the land of the living. Teach me the imaginative language of the Spirit. Open my eyes to ee, and activate my spirit to discern the presence of the angelic realms. Teach me how to engage and dispatch the invisible realm of angels to advance Your Kingdom. I ask that the Spirit of Truth lead and guide me into all truth! Amen.

CHAPTER THIRTEEN

Fruitful Growth by Persevering

Perseverance empowers us to press onward in order to obtain an ever-increasing state of prosperity. We continue to move up into another expanded mansion by maintaining our present higher state of existence. While we continue to ascend, we transition into another mansion residing in the next higher state of Christ consciousness. Faith is the fabric that clothes our desires while we are in the process of being changed into its image. Always remember: *The Lord your God is in your midst, a mighty one who will save; He will rejoice over you with gladness; He will quiet you by His love; He will exult over you with loud singing* (Zephaniah 3:17).

> *Grace and peace be multiplied to you in the knowledge of God and of Jesus our Lord, as His divine power has given to us All Things that pertain to life and godliness, through the knowledge of Him who called us by glory and virtue, by which have been given to us exceedingly great and precious promises, that through these you may be partakers of the divine nature, having escaped the corruption that is in the world through lust. But also, for this very reason, giving all diligence, add to your faith virtue, to virtue knowledge, to knowledge self-control, to self-control perseverance, to perseverance godliness, to godliness brotherly kindness, and to brotherly kindness love. For if these things are yours and abound, you will be neither barren nor unfruitful in the knowledge of our Lord Jesus Christ. For he*

who lacks these things is shortsighted, even to blindness, and has forgotten that he was cleansed from his old sins. Therefore, brethren, be even more diligent to make your call and election sure, for if you do these things you will never stumble; for so an entrance will be supplied to you abundantly into the everlasting kingdom of our Lord and Savior Jesus Christ (2 Peter 1:2–11).

Perseverance is a key to obtaining what one desires or imagines. The Bible is full of examples of people who persevered through difficult, impossible situations in order to receive from God. We are told to ask and keep on asking, to seek and keep on seeking and knock and continue to knock until the door opens to grant us access. Allow me to give several biblical illustrations.

Prophet Elisha

"Tarry here, I pray you, for the Lord has sent me to Bethel, then to Jericho and finally to the Jordan area to visit my three schools of the prophets." But each time Elisha was asked to stay put, Elisha replied, "As the Lord lives and as your soul lives, I will not leave you on any of these trips."

So, they both went down to three different schools of the prophets that were located at Bethel, in Jericho and also in the Jordan River area. At each of these respective schools, Elisha was told each time, "The Lord is going to take your master Elijah away to heaven today." But the prophet Elisha persevered, even when Elijah told him to stay behind. Elijah stated, "As the Lord lives and as your soul lives, I will not leave you" (2 Kings 2:2–6).

The Widow's Oil

The widowed wife of the sons of the prophet came to Elisha saying, "My husband that feared the Lord is dead. What shall I do? The creditors are coming to take my two sons (promises) *as slaves to pay off my debt!" Elisha asked her, "What type of resources dwelt within her personal house or 'body.' What do you have of value in the house?" She was aware of a few small drops of oil in a jar* (represents the anointing of joy that produces an inner strength). *She responded, "Nothing except a jar of oil!"* Our awareness of even a small drop of joy that is resident within us, when focused upon, will spring up like an oil well. The oil well will overflow like a river, filling every vessel or person around us. The river of God fills people to the full, then to overflow so that they sow back into us ensuring that we prosper too.

Elisha said, "Go gather all the empty vessels you can borrow from your neighbors. Shut yourself in with your sons. Shut the door on your emotions of fear and grief, and pour out your anointing of joy until every vessel is full. Then keep pouring out the oil as it multiplies into the vessels you have borrowed until each one is full. When the last vessel was filled, the flow of oil ceased, because the need had been met. Then Elisha commissioned the widow to, "Go, sell the oil and pay your debt; and you and your sons shall live on the abundance that is left over" (2 Kings 4:1–7).

So many times, people's prayers go unanswered, because they pray without faith or for something that goes against God's creative principles and biblical ways. For example, Even though I am praying to be healed, yet I have focused all of my energy and consciousness on the pain caused by my diseased body, I will receive what IAM already conscious of being, which is a pain-filled state of dis-ease. Even though I pray and beg God to make me rich, yet IAM constantly conscious of being in a state of poverty, I can only receive that which I believe myself to be, which is poor. I must change the image I see of myself. I must believe that IAM transformed into a new, healthy and prosperous being.

To do this, I must go within to the secret place and shut the door to the outer world that I was once aware of battling. I need to then claim and continue to manifest the new, desired state as mine. I do this by denying my physical senses rather than begging God to do something that violates my conscious will. God gladly rewards me for the conviction of things that I have consciously done and desired in secret. Tell no one but the three-in-one God your secret; for people may discourage your faith.

Jesus said He is the way, the truth and the life. No one comes unto the Father, who grants us the awareness of being in Christ, except by the consciousness of Him. This is why we are told to seek the Kingdom of God first, then All Things that we desire and decree shall be established and added unto us.

God speaks to us according to the desires of our imagination. When we act on the desire of our heart as if we have already possessed the state of its fulfillment, we bring the state we long for into existence. When the widow and her sons assumed a higher state of joy, they were no longer poor, existing in a weakened state of fear, lack and poverty. The widow learned how to use what was already in her home to preserver and get out of debt.

> *When we act on the desire of our heart as if we have already possessed the state of its fulfillment, we bring the state we long for into existence.*

Will not our loving God speedily defend, avenge and protect His elect chosen ones who continually cry out to Him day and night in prayer? Yes, He will defend and protect His Believers. However, when the Son of Man comes, will He find persistent perseverance in faith on the earth (see Luke 18:1–8)?

The following parables taken from the Bible serve as excellent examples and teachings that illustrate faith, persistence and perseverance. All of these individuals had to imagine a different outcome to the life situation they were living through. They had to know the answer was present and believe that their deliverance was real. They had to believe that the healing of their loved ones had surely manifested. They had to see the end result, hold onto it and then cause it to manifest into their now.

> *Keep on asking and it will be given you; keep on seeking and you will find; keep on reverently knocking and the door of opportunity will be opened to you. For everyone who keeps on asking receives; and he who keeps on seeking finds; and to him who keeps on knocking, the door Jesus will be opened* (Matthew 7:7–8).

The Prophet-Honoring Woman

The rich, influential, barren Shunamite woman made a small chamber with a bed, table, chair and lamp on the roof of her housetop for the Prophet Elisha, so whenever Elisha came through Shunem, he could turn in to eat, rest and sleep. Elisha prayed for her to bear a son the following year.

When the son had grown, he went with his father to reap in the field. The lad suffered from sunstroke that hurt his head so bad the servants carried him home to his mother. He sat on her knees till noon and then died. She went up and laid her son on Elisha's bed and shut the door upon him and went out. And she called to her husband and said, "Send me one of the servants and one of the donkeys that I may go quickly to the man of God and come back again." And he said, "Why go to him today?" And she said, "It will be all right." She saddled the donkey, set out for Elisha and said to her servant, "Ride fast; do not slacken your pace for me unless I tell you."

Elisha saw her afar off. He sent his servant Gehazi to meet the Shunammite, asking, "Is it well with you? Well with your husband? Well with the child?" And she answered, "It is well." When she came to Elisha, she persevered and clung to his feet. Gehazi came to thrust her away, but the man of God said, "Let her alone, for her soul is bitter and vexed within her, and the Lord has hidden the reason for her urgency from me and has not told me." Then she said, "Did I desire a son of my lord? Did I not say, 'Do not deceive me?'"

The prophet Elisha said to Gehazi, "Get ready to run and take my staff in your hand and go lay my staff (conduit of power and rod of authority) on the face of the child. If you meet any man, do not salute him (acknowledge or make any contact). If he salutes you, do not answer him (defuse or dilute the power you carry)." The mother of the child persevered. She said, "As the Lord lives and as my soul lives,

I will not leave you." And he arose and followed her.

Gehazi passed on as he ran before them. He laid the staff on the child's face, but the boy neither spoke nor heard. So he went back to meet Elisha and said to him, "The child has not awakened."

When Elisha arrived in the house, the child was dead and lain upon his bed. So Elisha went in, shut the door on the two of them and continually prayed to the Lord. Elisha persevered as he went up and lay on the child, put his mouth on his mouth, his eyes on his eyes and his hands on his hands. He persevered as he stretched himself on him and embraced him until the child's flesh became warm again. Then the Prophet Elisha returned and walked back and forth in the house. He persevered and went up again and stretched himself upon him. And the child sneezed seven times, blowing death out of the seven life centers and vital organs in his body, and then he opened his eyes. Elisha called to Gehazi who called the Shunammite, so that she could take up her living son (see 2 Kings 4:8–38).

The Desperate Mother

A Syrophoenician woman whose little daughter was under the control of an unclean, demonic spirit heard about Jesus so she came to Him, flung herself down and clung onto His feet. She persevered as she continued to beg Jesus to drive the demon out of her daughter. She was not offended when Jesus said, "First let the children be fed, for it is not becoming or proper or right to take the children's bread and throw it under the table to the little house dogs."

She persisted and answered Him, "Yes, Lord, yet even the small pups under the table lick up and eat the little children's scraps of food."

Jesus said to the Gentile woman, "Because of your perseverance, you may go your way; the demon has permanently gone out of your daughter." When she arrived home, she found the child thrown on the couch, and the demon departed (see Mark 7:25–30).

Jesus told the desperate mother that her faith-filled, perseverance had insured that the demon could not come back into her daughter. This is profound because often people who are healed or delivered will return to their sin, doubt or unbelief, giving the demon or disease the right to reenter and take up residence again.

A Mercy-Seeking Father

The father of the moonstruck, epileptic son persisted when he came to Jesus to ask for Him to pity and have mercy on his son. He said, "Because of his terrible suffering, he frequently falls into the fire and many times into the water when the demons try to kill him. I brought him to Your disciples, but they were not able to cure my son."

Jesus answered, "You unbelieving, perverse, wayward, rebellious generation! How long am I able to remain with you? How long am I to bear with you? Bring your epileptic son to Me." Jesus rebuked the demon, and it came out of the boy who was instantly cured.

The disciples came privately to Jesus to ask, "Why couldn't we drive the demon out?" Jesus replied, "It is because of your little faith, a lack of firm, God-like truth, and this kind of demon does not go out except by prayer and fasting" (see Matthew 17:14–21).

The Persistent Widow

The parable of the unjust judge illustrates that we ought to pray always and never faint. We are not to be cowardly. We are not to lose heart. We are never to give up on anything we desire to accomplish. This certain judge neither feared nor reverenced God, nor did he respect or consider any person important.

There was a widow in that same city who persevered in her coming to the judge, seeking his protection and defense to give

> *her justice against her adversary. For a time, the judge would not help the widow, but because she continued to bother him, she persevered in her pursuit. So the unjust judge decided, "I will defend, protect and avenge her lest her intolerable annoyances wear me out with her continual, nonstop persistence. If I don't do something on her behalf, she may rail on me, assault or strangle me"* (Luke 18:3–8).

The double-minded person is controlled by the spasmodic demons of fear. These unclean spirits burn pessimistic and depressing thoughts into the mind. Critical, judgmental thoughts plunge people into a perverse, hopeless state of disbelief. Their energy is turned into a vortex of confusion, so they sabotage and defeat themselves by making the wrong decisions and taking the wrong actions.

To obtain our deliverance and also facilitate the healing of others, we must truly know that our faith is based in the working power of God. Knowing that we possess the same resurrection power and authority that raised Christ from the dead gives us the same abilities that Jesus has in the realm of the Spirit. Believers are able to work in tandem with the Holy Spirit and a troop of resurrection angels to raise the dead too!

Let Us Pray

Dear heavenly Father, I ask that You clothe me in the fabric of Your great faith to make my calling and election sure. Multiply grace and peace to me in the knowledge of God so that I may exercise more self-control and preserver in godliness. Then I can obtain the things I have imagined. Increase my measure of glory and virtue so that I can ascend and take up residence in a higher spiritual mansion. Prepare me to apprehend the precious promises You have given to me so that I may be a partaker of Your divine nature. I long to escape the corruption that is in this world through lust.

Lord Jesus, I ask that You speak to me according to the desires You have placed within the heart of my imagination. Empower me to keep on seeking, asking and knocking so that I can receive from the doors that are opened to me in Your heart. Amen.

CHAPTER FOURTEEN

Creative Transformation

The creative miracle of transformation takes place by filling our bodies with the living water of the Word of God and by releasing our expressions of love toward God.

The Woman at the Well

In biblical times, a Jewish man would have never broken social barriers to confront or approach a woman, especially a Samaritan woman, much less ask her for a drink of water. The only women men addressed in public were prostitutes, fortunetellers and prophetesses.

> Jesus came to a well where a Samaritan woman was drawing water in the heat of the day. He asked her for a drink. The Samaritan's response to Jesus' favorable question was one of surprise. "How is it that You, being a Jew, ask a drink of water from me, a Samaritan woman?"
>
> Jesus answered, "If you knew the inspirational gift of God's divine guidance, and Who it is Who says to you, 'Give Me a drink,' you would have asked Him for something much greater, and He would have given you living water that could breathe eternal life, which is the creative essence of God's light and infinite intelligence into you."

Jesus represented the four-dimensional, spiritual man who sees and knows everything about everyone's past, present and future. Jesus shifted the woman's thinking from the realm of natural limitations into the divine spiritual realm of possibilities.

The Samaritan woman represented the natural, three-dimensional, physical world that is dominated by the soul's mind, thought, will and emotional limitations. She was focused on Jesus' physical limitations, the fact that Jesus did not have a cup, bucket or rope by which to retrieve the thing He desired, which was a drink of water.

> As a prophetess, she inquired of Jesus about spiritual things, "Are you greater than our father Jacob (who used his physical senses to discern, bless and build), who gave us the well?" Jesus's response to her question was, "Whoever drinks of this well's natural water will thirst again, but whoever drinks of Me in the Spirit of Truth shall never thirst but have an internal, everlasting well springing up from within."

> Then Jesus amazed her by telling her how she had lived and made decisions in the past. To drive this point home, He requested that she go call her husband. She responded, "I have no husband." Jesus agreed with her statement and acknowledged that she had actually had five husbands (relying on her five natural senses) that she had submitted to and had been influenced by in the past. Jesus pointed out that the sixth husband that she was courting had not yet been actualized as an intimate husband. She had not taken on the sixth one's name, image or likeness, which would make them one through a covenant marriage.

Jesus, in essence, told her that the person she would like to be had not yet come into being. Her five natural senses had always denied her the ability to step into the Spirit to believe and see that she could be anyone other than who she had always been.

> Her response was, "I know that Messiah is coming to tell us All Things!" Jesus replied, "You do not have to wait any longer. The time is NOW; it has come. IAM the Messiah

who speaks to you!"

The disciples returned from buying food and found Jesus talking to the Samaritan woman. They invited Jesus to eat the food they bought. Jesus told them, "I have meat and drink you know not of. The food I have that keeps Me going is to do the will of the Father who sent Me by finishing the work He started."

Then the Samaritan woman perceived that Jesus was the IAM—a prophet, the Bread of Life, the Living Water, the Meat of the Word, the Wine—because He could tell her about her inner contemplations. She questioned Jesus about how and where to worship. Jesus told her, "You worship what you do not know, guessing in the dark about things you do not understand. The Jews have made God's way to salvation available. But now is the hour in time when as true worshippers we will worship the Father in Spirit and in Truth. God is Spirit, and those who follow, adore and worship Him must do so in a spirit of holiness and by living a life full of His truth."

Having received Jesus as her Messiah, she left her waterpot (the old, limited measure and way of doing things) and returned to the village to publicly tell the people that she had found the Messiah. She told them, "He is the giver of salvation who knew me inside and out. I drank of His eternal, living water" (see John 4:7–29).

When the Samaritan woman was approached by Jesus' salvation, she was immediately transformed. She changed from being a woman who thought in a limited way, accepting the physical reasons of why she could not do something, or be someone different. She immediately stopped postponing her new identity until some far-off future time. She became a Believer, living in the now possibilities of her spiritual reality. She then evangelized the whole town inviting each one of them to come meet Jesus for themselves.

Personal Reflection Moment

As you look around in the natural right now,

> wouldn't you say that in about four months it will be time to harvest?
>
> Well, I'm telling you to change the way you view things.
>
> Open your spiritual eyes, and take a good look at what's already right in front of you. There are people and opportunities for change in every field that are ripe to harvest NOW!

When our spirit, soul and body are full of the supernatural Word of God, the presence of Jesus Christ in our earthen body changes the water into the new wine of joy that flows up into us from another, superior dimension. *For the whole earth will be filled to brimming over with the intimate living knowledge of the Lord Jesus just as water swells the sea, and the great ocean's depths and widths span the globe* (Isaiah 11:9).

The first archetype of prophetic transformation came at the Wedding of Cana through the six stone water pots that were used to wash and cleanse one self. These six vessels represent the number of man's weakness, toil or labor, where we wrestle with our carnal, physical world of humanity in order to enter into our higher spiritual natures.

The pure water was poured in until it filled up every place in the pot. The water continued to pour until it brimmed over. The creative Words of a loving God invited the creative miracle of transformation to take place. The invited, welcomed presence of Jesus at a covenant wedding ceremony transformed the pure water into the new wine. In order to be transformed, to be the best, we must be emptied of the old, open to the new, clean and pure and stand righteous in God's presence.

God's Spirit heals the functions of our bodies with a divine, supernatural manifestation of the power of love.

Transformation comes when you are actively obedient to God by serving others with your best gifts. Taste the sweet wine of the Holy Spirit. See to it that the Lord's goodness is released into and through you.

Faith is NOW! Faith comes from hearing the Word and seeing the Living Word of God in action. Dreams that are interpreted by prophetic words shift us from the past into the present so that our faith can boldly apprehend the future. To operate in the miracle realm, we have to shift into a higher state of consciously believing that which we see, say and hear in the Spirit. This instantly changes things in the creative realm of faith.

The creative, invisible realm of the Spirit revokes and instantly overrides and changes natural laws. The power of the Spirit recreates by overlapping or re-scripting the natural realm with the higher laws of the Spirit. God's Spirit heals the functions of our body with a divine, supernatural manifestation of the power of love. All fear, anxiety, depression and dis-ease are cast out by perfect love. This creative realm of the Spirit causes the human body, which is mostly water, to realign at a cellular level. The demons and dis-ease are removed, driven into dry, aired places, which makes room for the light of God's healing power, peace, prosperity and wholeness to enter in and take their place. The presence of God's Spirit neutralizes a fearful, wavering double mind, replacing one's instabilities with a sound mind that is focused upon the existence of Christ Jesus.

Let Us Pray

Dear Jesus, fill me with Your Word so that Your glory will explode in me, exude out of me and cause me to carry Your glory all over the world. Transform me into a new creature in Christ. Empty me of all my old ways that are not pleasing unto You. Cleanse my hands, and purify the heart of my imagination so that I may be filled with new, sweet wine. Recreate in me a desire to override the natural laws by re-scripting my heart with the higher laws of the Spirit. I want to experience Your perfect love in order to cast out all fear, anxiety, depression and disease. Realign me at the cellular level to remove everything from me that is not of You. Amen.

CHAPTER FIFTEEN

God's Answer for Healing

God gave Moses the regulations for any diseased person at the time of their ceremonial cleansing, when they were brought to the priest (see Leviticus 14). The priest or person ministering healing to him or her own self or others who were sick or afflicted was told to take two birds.

Birds symbolize messengers of blessing, thoughts or ideas, spiritual gifts or evil, disease or curses. A bird can represent a person's thoughts that quickly fly by or come to rest, or it can represent an idea that is received and incubated as an egg that hatches, grows and matures to take flight. Birds are considered good or evil depending upon their type, colors, nature and characteristic actions.

The Holy Spirit is pictured as a peaceful, gentle dove, while a vulture represents an unclean, selfish schemer who has a fleshly appetite that benefits from the mistakes of others. Vultures take from others and feed on deadly, vile words that bring decay, sickness and death. The double-minded person has two different birds (ideas or trains of thought). One bird is of faith and prosperity, while the other bird is of doubt and unbelief, leading to sickness and poverty. The erratic person continues to go back and forth between these two opinions, which causes them to become unstable in all their ways. People see themselves as they are conscious of currently being defined by their natural senses. They also see themselves as the different person they would hope to become in the future. One bird represents the problems, weakness, lack and shortcomings, while the other conceptualized person's bird sees the answer and solutions to their problems by faith.

If the person is sick or diseased, the answer is healing and deliverance through the life-giving, saving blood of Jesus. Blood gives life. So kill the bird of disease by removing your conscious focus from it, thus draining its lifeblood. If you are poor or lacking, stop focusing on the problem of poverty. The answer to scarceness is centering on God's prosperity and abundant blessings. If you are bound to a sin that has imprisoned you, the solution is repentance. Focus your lifeblood on being set free from deprivation by coming into the liberty of the Spirit. Kill the problem bird by draining its lifeblood from it. Dip the living bird or answer to your previous problem into the sacrificial blood of the dead bird, which represents a negative idea, sickness, disease or an adverse situation.

> *We fear that if we prophesy that God is doing it NOW, instead of later, He won't show up to perform.*

We are told to be sprinkled in the blood seven times in order to be cleansed, delivered or healed. Seven is the perfect number of God's Sabbath rest, but it also represents vulnerability. Consistently thinking of being in your new, healed state and continually resting there will prevent the returning of evil. Stop thinking about your past condition or problem. Decree your deficiency is over, done and finished.

Now set the living bird free! Let your new identity grow, emerge and take flight. Feel that you have received your answer and have been set free, healed or delivered. Become a new creation, and take on your new identity of being a new creature in Christ. Allow the answer to your problem to take flight. Gratefully receive your desired state of being. Now let your spirit ascend into the heavenlies. The perfect image that was seen manifesting in heaven is now released to transform the person who needs healing, deliverance or any other kind of emotional, spiritual, physical or reconstructive creative miracle.

Believers are called Believers because they believe that All Things are possible through Christ Jesus' love, which strengthens them in the power of His might! The future becomes the now when the focus of the imagination becomes a presently seen reality. Seeing through God's eyes of love activates our faith into believing like God believes so that All Things become possible. Difficult circumstances are transformed into opportunities when we manifest the wisdom of what we have seen in the visionary realms. It is by faith that we bring the positive changes that we have only glimpsed in the Spirit realm into our natural existence.

The power of a creative imagination works best when the Believer creates miracles by utilizing the faith of God. People only prosper a little when they relate to God through a small measure of faith that is based on only hearing others tell secondhand stories about God. Job admitted to God, *I have only heard of You by the hearing of the ear, but now my own eye sees You* (Job 42:5).

Believing that what the Word of God says is true empowers us to tear down the altars we have erected to honor false gods. The power of His living Word endows us with the decision-making power to rid ourselves of the powerless traditions imposed on us by a religious society. Viewing life from a Christ-centered state of being and seeing the end from the beginning elevates the Believer into a heavenly platform. When we are resting in Christ, we rule over situations from a heavenly perspective instead of having to blindly fight in the dark or struggle while being under a heavy cloud of opposition.

Man's ignorance of God's love, power and creative ways holds people captive to one narrow strain of thought or natural pattern of response. In order to broaden ourselves and free ourselves from bondage, we must believe, see and activate our faith to move in the acts of power that come from a higher level of reality. Faith produces a positive spiritual atmosphere that forces natural changes in our personal being and in our physical environment.

> *Prayer is the power that creates the double doors that we open to release everything in the realm of the Spirit to manifest on earth according to Christ's riches in glory.*

Two of the greatest gifts Christ gave to humanity are our imagination and our vocal ability to pray, prophesy and decree into existence whatever we believe, touch, hear and see in the realm of the Spirit. *When He ascended on high, He led captivity captive, and gave gifts to men* (Ephesians 4:8). God sees and relates to us in our mature, finished spiritual condition. *He who descended is also the One who ascended far above all the heavens, that He might fill All Things* (Ephesians 4:10).

Prayer is a powerful force that can save an individual, a whole nation and even the entire world from destruction. Prayers for righteousness (right standing or aligned under God's ways and laws) and justice will remold and change a nation's destiny (reference to Esther's account in Volume III). Prayer exposes and destroys the wicked schemes of political darkness. Prayer defeats evil and assures the righteous, godly candidate wins the election. Faith-filled prayer averts disaster and prevents tragedies from happening.

Prayer is the power that creates the double doors that we open to release everything in the realm of the Spirit to manifest on earth according to Christ's riches in glory. Prayer is like a magnet that energizes and activates the glory realm. The biblically-based words of our prayers release things in the Spirit by attracting to us everything we need. Prayer draws heavenly wisdom and the answers we seek into a realm where we can access them by faith. Prayer activates us to function in the power of God's might.

When we prayerfully invite and desire God's presence, *All Things* shall be added unto us. *Blessed are those who hunger and thirst for righteousness, for they shall be filled* (Matthew 5:6). Once we are filled with the Spirit of God, the next phase is stepping into the overflowing presence of more than enough. Now we have all that we need, so the surplus can be sown into the needs of others.

God told me that He wants His prophets to believe His Word. God wants prophets to start exaggerating their prophetic words so that God has a broader, more glorious entrance onto a grander stage. He wants His prophets to boldly stand up within the united Body of Christ to perform miracles. Sadly, we have limited God by our narrow, natural interpretations that are full of doubt or unbelief. Doubt-filled prayers, prophecies and declarations of, "God, if it be Your will," when the Word of God clearly states the full will of God, introduce doubt and unbelief into the situation. These types of prayer and prophecies conveniently postpone

> *The hope of obtaining glory inspires us to rise above the ordinary to become our highest possible redeemed person.*

God's arrival to some distant or future time.

We prophesy delay by declaring, "God is going to…," instead of stating, "He has already done it! Instead of declaring, "He is here now!," we prophesy a stay of God's hand, because we want to be safe. We fear that if we prophesy that God is doing it NOW that He won't show up to perform. Because we have not spent the time necessary to visually establish it in prayer, we do not really believe that it will appear, we do not boldly declare the miracle, or the answer to the problem, which, if we did believe, would shatter the darkness or release the light of wisdom. The doubt-filled words that form the impediment also prove that we don't believe God will show up right now to honor and fulfill His Word.

Set a new standard of excellence in your life. Cut off all of the things that hinder your progress or weigh you down.

We must stop trying to protect our reputations. Jesus made Himself of no reputation. We must remember that Faith is NOW! Faith, by its very nature, requires that we be willing to take a risk and confidently place everything we believe on the line! Scripture states, Now is the acceptable time of salvation, for Emanuel is always with us, causing the kingdom of heaven that is currently within us to be at hand (see 2 Corinthians 6:2; Matthew 28:20; Matthew 10:7).

If we are born again, the Savior has already come. He appears to us, and He is continually dwelling within us. If we deny God's modern-day omnipresence before men, stating that He will soon come and appear, Jesus will deny that we are saved before His Father (see Matthew 10:33). Signs follow those who believe that they are currently saved by Christ's ever-existing presence dwelling within.

If we practice our religious, traditional beliefs in a spirit of fear, doubt and unbelief, we continually nullify the power of God. Jesus called forth the greater works generation to arise, to do exceedingly and abundantly above all we can desire, ask or hope for in our highest prayers, all that we can think in our thoughts, all that we can dream or imagine. *All Things* according to the measure of His power that is working within us (see Ephesians 3:20). We retain the authority to influence others through spiritual intervention.

We can progress by changing the level of concepts that we currently possess about ourself. In order to experience a much higher self-concept and advance, we trade in the lesser. We limit Jesus to the measure of His creative power (the imagination) that is working within us. To gain a greater vision or measure of power working in us, we need to focus our attention on seeking the Kingdom of God first. Focusing on the Kingdom causes us to tap into the unlimited supply of the God kind of faith that is found in the Christ-centered, awakened imagination. Then *All Things* that we ask for in faith will manifest when we focus our attention on creating our ideal dream.

The world was formed by God's creative imagination. Jesus entered the very world He created, yet the world was completely unaware of His presence. Jesus is the Life Light of the world. He brings His eternal light into the world through each and every Believer. The whole world was made through Jesus, yet the world did not know Him. *For it is the God who commanded light to shine out of darkness, who has shone in our hearts to give the illuminating light of the knowledge of the glory of God in the face of Jesus Christ* (2 Corinthians 4:6).

Christ gives to those who believe that He dwells in them the power to become their true, enlightened and glorious selves, their begotten child of God selves. Your dreams and imagination give you the creative power that is necessary to remold your world by accessing the thing that Christ has placed deep within your very being. The hope of obtaining glory inspires us to rise above the ordinary to become our highest possible, redeemed person.

> To gain a greater vision or measure of power working in us, we need to focus our attention on seeking the Kingdom of God first.

Our dreams and desires are determined by the present needs in our life. We tend to keep objective, outward focuses on external circumstances. But when we place our attention on God, He directs our subjective, spiritual inner focus. Once we realize that it is Christ living within us that controls our imagination, we will stop relying on the outside circumstances of the world. If our one aim in life is to totally embrace the grandeur of our all-powerful God, He will flow out of us to manifest in ways we have never seen before. *And whatever you do, do it heartily, as to the Lord and not to men*

(Colossians 3:23).

God holds us to a much higher standard of excellence than that of man. When we passionately thirst after God and His righteousness, like the deer that pants for the refreshing water brook, our desire to breathe in God's presence will cause us to prosper (see Psalm 42:1). Pursuing our life's passions makes us a more captivating person. The spiritually enlightened person is both delightful and mesmerizing.

Before we ask, God has already set the answer in motion. When we accept the end results as our current truth, we will realize the visible manifestation of it in our waking life. When our spirit is submitted and connected to the Holy Spirit, our prayers, prophecies and spiritual decrees will empower our soul to surrender to the leading of our spirit. Put your trust in God's saving, healing light while you have access to it.

> *The eye is the lamp of the body; so, then if your eye is clear, your whole body will be full of light. But if your eye is bad, your whole body will be full of darkness. If then the light that is in you is darkness, how great is the darkness* (Matthew 6:22–23)*!*

Set a new standard of excellence in your life. Cut off all of the things that hinder your progress or weigh you down. Stop being friends with the world. Develop an intimate relationship with Jesus, the eternal Lover of your soul.

The night is almost finished. The day is almost here, so we should stop doing whatever belongs to darkness. We should prepare ourselves to fight evil with the weapons that belong to the light. We should live in a right way, like people who belong to the day. We should not have wild parties or be drunk. We should not be involved in sexual sin or any kind of immoral behavior. We should not cause arguments and trouble or be jealous. Be like the Lord Jesus Christ, so when people see what you do, they will see Christ. Don't think about how to satisfy your sinful self or the bad things you want to do. Don't criticize others. Be willing to accept those who still have doubts about what Believers can do. And don't argue with them about their different ideas (see Romans 13:12–14).

The renewing of the mind empowers the Believer to advance from good efforts to acceptable behaviors, then from acceptable behaviors to fulfilling the perfect will of God. *Examine me, O Lord, and prove me; try my mind and my heart* (Psalm 26:2). The life of the Believer is to prove or demonstrate the perfect will of God by manifesting the kingdom of heaven on earth. *As for God, His way is perfect; the Word of the Lord is proven; He is a shield to all who trust in Him* (Psalm 18:30).

When Believers walk in the perfect will of God, the windows of heaven open in order to fill the mansions of God with fresh bread, solid meat and the heavenly manna of revelation. The individual body of Believers is the windows, gateways, portals and living temples and houses in the many mansions of God! *"And prove Me now in this," says the Lord of hosts, "If I will not open for you the windows of heaven and pour out for you such blessing that there will not be room enough to receive it"* (Malachi 3:10–12).

Let Us Pray

Dear Jesus, You are my Savior, Healer and Deliverer. I place all of my trust in You alone. I ask that You help me take authority over every thought of my mind so that I can take captive and cast down every vain, sick or negative imagination. I ask that the Holy Spirit descend, rest upon and take up residence within me. I evict, slay and remove any other predatory, devouring bird that would try to nest within my mind. I dismantle every destructive nest and remove all access to my mind. I now see, believe and activate my God-given faith in order to move into more acts of power and from a higher level of reality. I speak, decree, declare, pray and prophesy with words of authority the things I have seen in my imagination to activate the glory realm.

Help me to prophesy a now word of faith so that You can come on the season whenever You desire. Help me to manifest by faith that ideal dream You have given to me. As You have become my life light, let Your light within me arise and shine for the world to see. Help me to achieve my one aim in life to totally embrace the grandeur of the all-powerful God so that He can flood through me and manifest in ways the world has never seen before. Empower me to prove and manifest the perfect will of God. Open the windows of heaven, and pour upon me a blessing I am not able to hold within, so I can pour it out on all those I meet. Amen.

CHAPTER SIXTEEN

The Imaginative Dreamer

The dreams, visions, prayer and prophetic words we decree give us the spiritual sights and divine direction that keep us connected to the purposes of heaven. God is eternal, so these avenues of revelation reveal the eternal plans God has for our continual advancement. The different states, dimensions or mansions of God are also eternal. God's strategic plans for us are eternally proceeding with no end in mind.

The salvation of a soul is a spiritual transformation. There is an induced spontaneous, dramatic metamorphic process that brings about revolutionary changes. A person is reshaped one characteristic, attribute or element at a time into another appearance, form or identity from a foundational cellular level. Every thought or idea produces a feeling. Those subconscious impressions and feelings birth a future action. While we are awake, we are busy collecting and selecting the seeds of wisdom that we will drop into the ground of our soul when we are asleep. These ideas and concepts that we plant will formulate the dreams that grow or produce the fruits we bring forth in our waking life.

The subconscious dreams (visions) we understand and apply become the doorways to heaven, and they make us conscious of God's will here on earth. *Most assuredly, I say to you, unless a grain of wheat falls into the ground and dies, it remains alone; but if it dies, it produces much grain* (John 12:24). This spiritual transfiguration liquidates our inner man, renews our mind and refines and reorganizes our thought patterns in order to reconstruct our being. Therefore, we resonate at a much higher spiritual frequency that manifests the love of God.

Joseph was an imaginative dreamer of dreams (see Joseph 36; 39–41). Joseph's father, Jacob, represented the spirit who supplanted Esau, the hairy outer man, of the carnal flesh. After Jacob wrestled with God, his hip joint was dislocated, which limited the function of his body. From then on, his flesh had great pain, which made his walk in the flesh very difficult. His name was changed from Jacob (the supplanter) to Israel because he finally learned not to lean upon his own understanding but, instead, to (in all of his ways) acknowledge and lean upon God.

> The dreams, visions, prayer and prophetic words we decree give us the spiritual sights and divine direction that keep us connected to the purposes of heaven.

The spirit always rises above and supplants or takes the place of the arm of flesh. The list of the people who supplanted the carnal nature of the flesh with the imaginations of the Spirit of God's greatness manifesting on earth goes on and on throughout history.

Israel was an awakened, mature and spiritually imaginative man. Israel loved his son Joseph more than his other sons. Israel's favorite son, Joseph, represented the expression of his collective knowledge and the wisdom of his old age. Divine wisdom and knowledge that are from above do not come by living a long time. Rather, they come by embracing the powers found in our awakened, inventive imagination.

When someone says that the things one is dreaming about doing are impossible, the imaginative dreamer always responds, "I have already seen it done! I know the truth because I have discovered the secret that All Things are possible with God!" Great discoveries come through those who dare to explore and reach for the hidden resources found in the outer recesses of their imagination.

Joseph's father had given him a beautiful, long-sleeved tunic coat of many vivid, rainbow colors. Coats represent mantles that cover, psychological moods that inspire and attitudes or imaginative ways of thinking that clothe the dreamer's thoughts, feelings and designs.

The coat's long sleeves covered Joseph's arms of flesh. Symbolically, this encouraged Joseph to imagine what he could accomplish if he moved by the revelation found in his spiritual life dreams of destiny, not by the strength and power of his own arm of the flesh. We advance in the Kingdom of God, not by might or by power but by the Spirit of the Lord. These covenant colors of the rainbow are cast from a brilliant cut of the white diamond that reflects the brilliant light rays of the manifold wisdom of God.

Joseph (means *increase the standard*) was an imaginative dreamer who was full of the senses of life, creative meditations and inspirational ideas. Joseph imagined himself as being extremely successful. He was determined to rise above and exceed the accomplishments of all of his brothers. Joseph knew that out of all of his siblings, he had a distinct destiny to achieve. Joseph knew how to activate the power of his feelings. He cultivated the images of success that were found in his visions. All great achievers are daydreamers. Reality is made up of everything you can imagine.

Joseph dreamed that he would rise above and rule over his eleven jealous, disapproving brothers. Joseph freely shared his feelings of superiority. He stated that his brothers' sheaves stood around his bundle of superior stalks, which took a high, prominent place on center stage. Joseph described in detail how all of their persons stooped and obeyed his every command. He announced that their bundle of resources bowed down to serve his sheaf. So his brothers retorted, *"Shall you indeed reign over us? Or are you going to have us as your subjects and dominate us?" And they hated and rejected him all the more for his dreams* (Genesis 37:8).

Joseph was totally devoted and committed to the things he imagined in his dreams. He lifted up his dreams and aspirations until the pictures became clear in his mind. Joseph was consciously aware of his desired circumstances.

Joseph knew he was called to be successful. He was created to rise to the top. Whatever he desired to accomplish; he knew that he would. Joseph was focused and determined to achieve his imminent destiny. To Joseph, being the leader of the family was already a fixed reality in his future. Jo-

> *The subconscious dreams (visions) we understand and apply become the doorways to heaven, and they make us conscious of God's will here on earth.*

seph remained faithfully focused until he felt that he was able to walk into his prestigious future one step at a time. A disciplined, noble imagination that practices godly concepts and principles will obtain the wisdom that is necessary to overcome every obstacle or limitation.

The Bible teaches that the members of our own household will be our enemies. In dreams, the pits, tents, houses, buildings, mansions or palaces that we reside within represent the inner thoughts or the various conditions that we find ourself in. Our own fearful, negative or adverse inner speech or critical thoughts, feelings, ideas and wrong beliefs can often easily oppose our progress. These destructive emotions can cast us into a crater of depression that totally defeats us. If we are not watchful, these personal enemies can rise up to fight against us. They raise their ugly heads to challenge, dispute and contradict us with the combative feelings that our particular aspirations or private dreams are impossibilities.

Our own fearful, negative or adverse inner speech or critical thoughts, feelings, ideas and wrong beliefs can often easily oppose our progress.

To rise above all of the internal voices and those of our brethren, which are the members of our own household, we must detach and separate ourself from their intrusive, negative influences. We, like Joseph, must stay focused on our goals and objectives by thinking positive, hope-filled, creative thoughts until our desires are seen, accessed and realized.

Joseph's deep, narrow and confining coffin was made from a rock pit. This stone casket served as the place where Joseph (imagination) died to self. While confined within the walls of the dry well, where he had been thrown by his covetous, resentful brothers, Joseph learned how to exercise the self-control that was necessary to discipline his imagination. While collapsed on the bottom of a hot, dirty pit floor, he began the metamorphic process of transformation to become the world's deliverer.

Joseph's life story demonstrates to us that the creative, life-giving imagination can solve any problem in the world. No matter how enormous or devastating the catastrophe appears to be, the imaginative dreamer can receive or invent the solution. God redefined Joseph's purposes when his jealous, desirous brothers captured and buried him alive in the depths of a hollow, cratered abyss. As an isolated seed, Joseph fell to the ground to be buried alone. When Joseph's transformation was complete, promotion to the highest possible position came to him as Pharaoh said to Joseph, *See, I have set you over all the land of Egypt* (Genesis 41:41).

Joseph was lifted from the pit and sold into Egypt as a slave. He rose to the top position in Potiphar's house. Then he was imprisoned on false accusations of sexual misconduct for many years before he was summoned to interpret Pharaoh's dreams. Great favor was given to Joseph. He reigned in the palace and over all of Egypt, second only to Pharaoh. This shows us that our thoughts, desires and goals must first go down; they must be subjected to Egypt. The Bible states, *Out of Egypt, I called My son* (Hosea 11:1; see Matthew 2:15).

We learn to overcome every obstacle in captivity before we can rise to a place of prominent leadership. God called Joseph from his tribal, desert family, where he was cast into the pit of jealousy. He was sold into years of bondage and slavery. He was lied about, defrauded and imprisoned for years for a crime he didn't commit. Before he could emerge as a free moral agent to rule next to Pharaoh in the palace, Joseph had to use his imagination to see how to prosper in every disparaging situation.

Joseph's imagination empowered him to become the favored ruler in every deprecating situation or belittling place he resided. Joseph continued to rise from the absolute bottom of a captive pit all the way to the prestigious, glamourous rule in a palatial Egyptian palace. His creative imagination gave him the visionary skills that were necessary to interpret the dreams of the lowly, imprisoned butler and baker. Joseph shed his slave clothes, washed, shaved and arose into a new identity. He boldly stood free and confident before the greatest Egyptian Pharaoh and interpreted his dreams. Joseph's imagination saved the world from the devastation of famine and the plague of death.

> *We learn to overcome every obstacle in captivity before we can rise to a place of prominent leadership.*

A disciplined, controlled imagination has the ability to rule over every concept, perception, impression and thought that is created in the mind. Joseph became the ruling commander in chief in every positive or negative venue and setting he encountered. Joseph was able to utilize his darkest times as a gestation period to birth creative ideas that would compel him into the liberating light of celebrated freedom. His prayers supplied him with the needed answers to become the head, not the tail.

The imaginative dreamer prospered because he didn't fall into self-pity and depression when problems arose. He held positive, creative attitudes that empowered him to overcome everything life threw at him. Joseph, the dreamer, cultivated his superior advisory skills and soared into Pharaoh's courts as the chief problem solver of a nation.

Jonah's Whale

The word of the Lord came to Jonah, "Arise, go to Nineveh, that great city, and proclaim against it; for their wickedness has come up before Me." But the prophet rose up and fled from the presence of the Lord to Tarshish, the most remote of the Phoenician trading places.

Jonah paid the fare, and he hid down into the belly of the ship. But the Lord sent a great wind and violent tempest upon the sea to break up the ship. The mariners on board were afraid and cried out to their gods. The sailors threw their cargo over into the sea to lighten their load while Jonah slept fast in the inner parts of the ship. The captain awoke Jonah and demanded he arise and call upon God! "Pray you, sleeper. Perhaps your God will give a thought to us so that we do not perish at sea."

The crew cast lots to determine why the evil had come upon them. The lot fell on Jonah. The men asked Jonah, "What is your occupation? Where did you come from? What is your country and nationality?"

Jonah replied, "I am a Hebrew prophet who fears and worships the God of heaven and earth, the One who made the seas and dry land."

The men cried out, "What have you done to us?" For Jonah had told them he had fled from being in the presence of the Lord. "What shall we do to cause the violent sea to subside and become calm again?"

Jonah said, "Take and cast me into the sea, and the tempest will become calm for you."

The men tried to row the ship to land, but they could not overcome the furious waves. They prayed to the Lord, "Please do not let us perish for this man's life, and do not lay the shedding of his innocent blood upon us." When they cast Jonah into the tumultuous sea, it became placid and calm. The crew reverently worshipped and feared the Lord, and they offered a sacrifice and made vows.

The Lord prepared and sent a great fish to rescue Jonah. The mouth of the massive whale swallowed Jonah alive, and he struggled, buried in its dark, flesh belly. Jonah was imprisoned, concealed there within that fish's stomach for three long days and three torturous nights. The putrid rot of flesh within the detaining gut chamber of the whale served as Jonah's transformational chrysalis.

Jonah prayed to the Lord from the great fish's belly, "In my distress I cried out of the belly of Sheol, and God heard me. Lord, You cast me into the depths of the heart of the seas, so the floods surrounded me; all of Your waves billowed over and bury me. I have been cast out of the sight of Your presence; yet I look toward You, imagining my deliverance. The waters in this fish's abyss belly surround me to extinguish my life. Seaweed wraps around my head to suffocate me. This whale plunged me to the very bottom roots of the mountain's caves, and the bars closed behind me forever. Yet, even there, I imagined, prayed to and remembered You, my source of mercy and loving kindness. You brought my fainted soul up to life from the pit of corruption. Those who do not know how to imagine Your greatness pay regard to false, useless idols, thus forsaking their only source of salvation. But as for me, I will gladly sacrifice all that I have in order to be restored to Your presence. I will think Your higher thoughts. I will imagine Your ways in order to follow You. I will pray, prophesy and decree Your answers with the voice of thanksgiving. I will pay homage to Your majesty, and I will remember and stay focused on that which I have vowed to do. My salvation and deliverance belong to the Lord!"

A disciplined, controlled imagination has the ability to rule over every concept, perception, impression and thought that is created in the mind.

When the Lord heard the repentant cries of Jonah's transformed heart, He spoke to the fish, and it vomited out Jonah upon the dry land (see Jonah 1–2).

Jael Nailed It!

The name Jael means *mountain goat*. Just like Jael, we will sweetly cover or blanket our weary enemy Sisera with the warm milk of hospitality until he falls asleep in peace. Then we will nail the skull of Golgotha (the place of death and carnal reasoning residing within our own tent or household) to the floor (see Judges 4:17-22).

The natural man will die and be buried there, but the spiritual man will resurrect to a new, creative and limitless life. When we leave that body of flesh and our five, natural senses behind, we will see, hear, feel and taste the warm milk of the Word. We will live and move and have our being in Christ Jesus, and we will be led by the Holy Spirit. We will follow God like Deborah, Barak and Jael as valiant warriors and as courageous, confident Sons and heroic, fearless Daughters of God.

God promises to supply all the things we need when we learn how to enter the realm of glory. We enter in by using a greater measure of His faith. But the things that we desire in life must be diligently pursued, sought after and worked for in order for us to obtain them.

Let Us Pray

Dear Holy Spirit, open my eyes to see and my heart to understand all of the dreams, visions, prayers and prophetic words You have given me that are full of Your spiritual insights, divine wisdom and heavenly purposes. Help me to embrace the divine wisdom and knowledge that is from above. Awaken my imagination to find Your inventive power. Let me advance through an enlarged measure of spiritual understanding. I will gladly sacrifice all that I have in order to be restored to Your presence. I will think Your higher thoughts. I will imagine Your ways in order to follow You. I will pray, prophesy and decree Your answers with the voice of thanksgiving. I will pay homage to Your majesty, and I will stay focused on that which I have vowed to do. My salvation and deliverance belong to the Lord! I ask that You, Mighty God, supply all of my needs according to Your riches in glory. Amen.

CHAPTER SEVENTEEN

Sons of God Arising

The Christ in us is the hope of glory that arises and shines forth out of us. We live and move and have our being in Christ Jesus.

> *Being then the children of God, we ought not to think that the divine nature is like gold or silver or stone, an image formed by the art and thought of man. Therefore having overlooked the times of ignorance, God is now declaring to men that all people everywhere should repent, because He has fixed a day in which He will judge the world in righteousness through a Man whom He has appointed, having furnished proof to all men by raising Him from the dead* (Acts 17:29–31).

The Sons of God will be sent into the world to preach the gospel with unprecedented signs, wonders and creative miracles following. *For the anxious longing of the creation waits eagerly for the revealing of the Sons of God* (Romans 8:19). The Sons of God live a life of privilege. They are granted all authority, all power and all knowledge. They are granted the might of heaven that flows through them according to their level of understanding of the revelation that is resting in Christ Jesus.

Like Elisha, who sealed up the heavens so that it did not rain for three and a half years, the Sons of God are arising to rule and rein the earth's economy, governments, geographic masses and atmospheres. The Sons of God will control weather patterns on earth through their ability to command the skies to become as their prayers and decrees are proclaimed in heaven. The prophet Elisha did double or twice the number of miracles as his mentor, Elijah. When our imagination is engaged and united with God's in the realm of the Spirit, we, as the One New Man, will have the capacity to see as God sees and to do as God says and does.

The Kingdom of God is filled with His glorious vision and perception. The Sons of God believe that they are what God says about them. They see themselves as God sees them, and they do what God commands. God's perception of us must become our focused reality. Knowing that God always has our very best in mind, we can rest at peace in His loving acceptance. Thankfully, God's love for us is not based on our performance. Before Jesus had done any miracles or great works, God praised, blessed and prophesied over Jesus, "This is My Beloved Son in whom IAM well pleased!"

> *The Sons of God believe that they are what God says about them. They see themselves as God sees them, and they do what God commands.*

We are created in God's image with a portion of His imagination to share in the communion of His Spirit. We have been given the ability to dream God's dreams, to hear His voice, to see His visions, to taste His goodness and to feel the intimate touches of His hands and the kisses of His mouth as we encounter Him as our loving Creator. A person's godly core values should never decrease but continually increase to promote prosperity through godly expansion. Wisdom never ends; it continues to grow and mature through the various times and seasons of God.

Believers in Jesus, as born-again Sons of God, can know and recognize God's divine wisdom and creative, miracle-working power in every aspect of their lives. The living power of God is resident within the Believer. Christ Jesus creates the images that He projects upon the screens of our imagination. God dreams inspire us to believe for and imagine greatness. These visual images give us the wisdom that is needed to live a richer, nobler, happier and love-fulfilled life of health, wealth and abundance.

When we focus on the presence of Christ within us, He arises and shows us glimpses of Himself. His ideas are received (pictured in our mind's eye), then acted upon in our subconscious thoughts. We are able to see how to invent whatever is needed. He gives us wisdom to correct any problem. Christ shares His knowledge with us so that we can resolve every impossible situation by following God's visionary blueprint.

> *For as many as are led by the Spirit of God, these are Sons of God. For you did not receive the spirit of bondage again to fear, but you received the Spirit of adoption by whom we cry out, "Abba, Father." The Spirit Himself bears witness with our spirit that we are children of God, and if children, then heirs—heirs of God and joint heirs with Christ, if indeed we suffer with Him, that we may also be glorified together* (Romans 8:14–17).

Everything in the world that has been created was once only a thought or an imagination in the eternal abode of man's heart. Inventions are fashioned to solve difficult problems that exist. The inventive ideas that Christ gives empowers us to create wealth that will make our lives more comfortable and finance the advancement of the Kingdom of God. The Spirit of Christ dwelling within the fearless heart of the Believer's imagination is the only true door to our reality.

Jesus is the author of pure imagination. He is the spiritual access door to every creative idea, image and component, because He is the Creator of All Things. Therefore, when we submit our creative imagination to Jesus Christ, His infinite intelligence can broaden our mystical understanding. Jesus enlightens our personal perceptions with His abundant, transcendent truth and wisdom.

> *The inventive ideas that Christ gives empower us to create wealth that will make our lives more comfortable and finance the advancement of the Kingdom of God.*

Once an idea appears as an image in our mind's eye, we can see it. By continually gazing upon it, we can bring it into clear focus in order to permanently capture that impression. By noticing all of its attributes, characteristics and dimensions, we are able to retain the imagination's suggestion by recording that thought in picture form. By focusing our attention on the image, it becomes a vivid, sustainable reality to us. When we have memorized the image, it is indelibility inscribed upon our heart, placed there as a precious treasured memory. To actualize this vision and bring it into the tangible realm of reality, we must learn how to draw its manifestation out of the spirit into our present world.

Once we open our imaginative eyes to look, we should also spend some time gazing within to continue to see the vision impressed upon our mind's eye. Once the vision is imprinted on us, we can continue to revisit that portion of revelation knowledge. Vision empowers us to retrieve the needed wisdom and information from our imagination at any time.

As soon as the idea or image has materialized within our imagination, we have etched it upon the tablet of our heart. This image is written within our memory; its impression becomes part of our being. Now that we see and recall that particular creative idea, powerful thought, illustration or aspect, it has been added to us. It is now a living part of us, and it will not disappear or fade into the past. If we are not able to walk in the full weight of the manifestation at that time, it will advance into the future and will be waiting for us there until we mature spiritually or come into that level of heavenly understanding.

The power of the subconscious can be used to create new ideas, form creative solutions or manufacture inventions that will draw financial success to us.

When the images in our prayers, dreams and visions become an active part of us, living as a captive thought in our imagination, we have taken possession of that creative idea or divine solution, profitable invention or broad structure. Now these graphic illustrations will continue to follow us throughout life and into the future. They are part of us because we have looked, discovered, seen, prophetically spoken, decreed, created and released them to manifest in our tangible world of reality.

The auditorium (the room or place in which you are currently located, or the vehicle that you are steering) always appears to be more real than the home, office, restaurant or mall that you just left or are on your way to. The present place that we inhabit *now* is more real to us than the office where we work or any other destination point. Yet we can still easily picture and instantly visit each of these previous locations by tapping into our vivid memories of them. What we want to see, what we see or what we remember seeing can be created, expanded and recreated or enhanced in our imagination. The brilliant colors on the pallet of the imagination can redesign, touch up or heal past memories, or they can skillfully paint a masterpiece of the future.

What we think or imagine is recorded in our memory. These wonderful memories have become a part of us that will last forever. God created us as immortal souls who live and move and have our being in Christ. We live in Christ. Therefore, we possess an imagination that will live during our lifetime and will continue to exist for all eternity. Designing destiny begins with the eyes of the imagination seeing impossibilities as possibilities. Then we pray to obtain what our will imagines and what our future self desires.

Christ's infinite intelligence has gifted us with many different concepts, designs or possibilities. Maybe He has given you an idea for a new book, a thriving corporation, a prosperous business, a needed invention or some other type of discovery.

The power of the subconscious can be used to create new ideas, form creative solutions or manufacture inventions that will draw financial success to us. The subconscious has the ability to fulfill the heart's desires for relationships with the right people, customers, associates or life partner.

We are made complete when we submit to the power of the Spirit of God dwelling within us. His presence keeps us fluid and whole so that we are not being fragmented, separated or divided into compartments. We become connected and joined as one with the Spirit of Christ living within us. It is the Spirit of Christ who heals and unifies the core of our consciousness.

By resting at a certain level in Christ, we will reside there until we decide to take up our bed and walk into a higher level of healing and transformational understanding.

The Christ within gives us the hope that we have of obtaining glory. We relate to God according to the way we see our own being and the concepts we believe about Him. God never changes. God always remains the same, while our conceptions, knowledge and beliefs about Him grow. We mature as our thoughts enter a higher realm of glory or mansion of understanding.

Believers evolve into Christ consciousness as we exit this natural realm to develop. The Spirit of Christ grants us an awareness of the myriad of different ways that God's wisdom functions. When we are enlightened, our whole person is unified so that we can commune within the oneness of God. Believers who trust in God the Father, God the Son and God the Holy Spirit become one with God. We become the temple of God, a living sacrifice or earthly habitation.

To hear, to see or to be touched by God, we must be in His presence. In His various dimensional auras, the Spirit of God emits different light forces. His abiding grace sustains the silence of tranquility that brings joy beyond description. In His peaceful, serene company, we are transformed into His resemblance. We become His earthly representation, living in Christ as One New Man.

The different characteristics, concepts and aspects of my personality do not arise out of three different persons. However, the various ways in which I present my being are all neighboring residences that live in the same body and consciousness of my one mind. The thoughts and ideas we ponder and the actions we take flow from the various arrangements of things that we believe are true. Every time we behold Jesus' coming in the Spirit, we are changed in His audience. Our spirit is awakened to live in a higher dimension. The Spirit easily touches and moves us. We are expanded. We have more of our being functioning in Christ's likeness.

> As Believers with the mind of Christ, we unite our sanctified imagination with the Holy Spirit in order to release the limitless Kingdom of God residing within us.

By resting at a certain level in Christ, we will reside there until we decide to take up our bed and walk into a higher level of healing and transformational understanding. To ascend to the next level of Christ consciousness, we have to rise and roll up our cot in order to go home, to the place Jesus has gone before to prepare for us. To move forward, we have to expand our knowledge of God. To ascend into a higher state of being, we have to repent. Changing the way we think and react breaks the restrictive cords that bind us to our current state of being. Only as we step into the new, are we able to leave the old behind in order to become unified as One New Man.

God has generously given us the incredible gift of imagination. The creative use of our imagination causes us to know Christ intimately, to reach our full potential, to fulfill fresh, God-directed purposes and to achieve our grand destiny. Christ has given Believers His wisdom, knowledge, revelation and creative power. Now is the time to courageously and passionately partner with God, to rise up as true Sons of God and as One New Man.

As Believers with the mind of Christ, we unite our sanctified imagination with the Holy Spirit in order to release the limitless Kingdom of God residing within us. We are able to successfully manifest God's majestic, supreme glory on earth as it is in heaven.

Now is the time to believe, dream, receive and take action. *Now* is the time to advance and achieve. Take flight and *imagine* the impossible, for nothing is impossible with God! God created you as a masterpiece, so imagine yourself as He sees you, without any limitations on who you can be, and with no restrictions on what you can have or achieve.

Let's Pray

Christ Jesus, You are the hope of the glory that arises and shines out of me. I live and move and have my being in You. My heart's desire is to be one of the Sons of God who are sent into the world to preach the gospel with unprecedented signs, wonders and creative miracles. I know that Your Word says I have been granted all authority, all power and all knowledge through Christ Jesus, my Lord. I humbly ask that You grant me more understanding of spiritual things and the mysteries of the Spirit so that I can flow in the revelation knowledge that come through resting in Jesus Christ, my Lord.

My heart's desire is to be part of the One New Man so that I will have the capacity to see as God sees and do as God says and does. Help me to believe what You say about me is true! Let me see the visual images that are inspired by God so that I can gain the wisdom that is needed for a richer, nobler, happier, love-fulfilled life of health and wealth in Christ. Grant me the access to the myriad of ways that Your wisdom functions. Change the way I think and respond. Break every cord of restriction so that I can ascend into a higher state of being to be with You where You are resting. Jesus, I have chosen You alone to be my inheritance. You are my great prize, my pleasure, my delightful reward and my abundant portion. I place the timing of the fulfillment of my complete destiny in Your capable hands (see Psalm 16:5). I awaken the living gates that are within me to rejoice. I command the ancient doors of my destiny to open wide and lift up their heads to declare the King of Glory has come in (see Psalm 24:7-9). Every moment of my life, my whole destiny is in Your loving hands. I know You alone can deliver me from those who relentlessly persecute and oppress me (see Psalm 31:15). Your sure plans for my destiny on earth stands true, they will forever remain in place and never fail (see Psalm 33:11).

The light of Your glory fell on me in Your sanctuary and vanquished my distorted perspectives. Now I understand that the destiny of the wicked is near (see Psalm 73:17). I thank you, Lord, that You have poured out so many amazing blessings on America, and You have restored Jacob's destiny from captivity (see Psalm 85:1) Those who choose to do wickedness die for lack of self-control. Their ignorant ways of foolishness lead them astray, delivering them as hostages of darkness and kidnapped prisoners robbed of their destiny (see Proverb 5:23). Those who seek to destroy America will only prosper and flourish for a moment. They foolishly forget their appointed destiny with death. If they do not repent, one day they will be destroyed forever (see Psalm 92:7).

I thank You that You give great skill to teach and make the immature wise, to give the youth of the world understanding of their grand design and great destiny in You (see Proverb 1:4). Thank you, Lord, for directing each step of my life, for All Things are ordained by You to bring me closer to my destiny. So much of my life remains a mystery, but You will shine Your light on my path (see Proverb 2:9).

The young will discover All Things just, proper and fair, and they will be empowered to make wise, upright decisions as they walk into the destiny You have created for them (see Proverb 2:9). The darkness of night has dissolved as a bright destiny dawn appears. So we must once and for all times strip away the shadows of darkness and burn up our filthy clothes. We must put on the brilliant garments of God's radiant light as a kingdom weapon (see Romans 13:12). A new day of destiny has dawned.

A new era is breaking forth all around me. I see the early signs of my purposes and plans budding and bursting forth. The vines are blooming, and the fragrant flowers whisper, "There is a change in the air." I will arise and seek after You with my whole heart that is full of love. As Your beautiful bride, IAM a grand champion who is not afraid to run to the battle or ascend to the high places to praise Your greatness (see Song of Songs 2:13). God, You have searched after my heart, and You know my longings. Yet You also understand the desires of the Holy Spirit's pleadings before God for me, His holy one, to come into perfect harmony with God's plans and purposed destiny for my life (see Romans 8:27). Having determined my destiny ahead of time, You have called me to Yourself. You have robed me in Your perfect righteousness, so IAM a co-heir with Jesus (see Romans 8:30).

God, nothing is impossible for You who achieved All Things and made it happen. It is You who guides the destiny of each generation from the beginning of time until now. You are the IAM, Yahweh, the Alpha and Omega, the unchanging Eternal One who will be here in the end (see Isaiah 41:4)! I hear the Lord saying, "IAM the One who gives you your destiny. IAM promising you the kingdom realm that My Father has promised Me (see Luke 22:29)." I know that this is not an empty hope, for God Himself is the very One who has prepared me from before the foundations of the earth for this wonderful destiny. He has given me the seal of the Holy Spirit, like a beautiful engagement ring, as a guarantee (2 Corinthians 5:5).

Through my blood-bought union with Christ, I, too, have been claimed by God as His own inheritance. Before I was even born He knew me and gave me my destiny, so I can fulfill the plans of God. And through the power of Christ working in me, I can accomplish every purpose and plan in His heart (see Ephesians 1:11). I have become His poetry, a recreated person that will fulfill the destiny He has given to me, for IAM joined to Jesus

Christ, the Anointed One. God planned in advance before I was born the very destiny and the good works I would do in His name (see Ephesians 2:10). IAM called as one body and one spirit to join with Jesus in the same glorious hope of divine destiny (see Ephesians 4:4). IAM convinced that any suffering I may endure is less than nothing compared to the magnitude of the glory that is about to be unveiled within me (Romans 8:18).

Therefore, I surrender my whole life to you, God. No one has the power to take my life from me. I have been given the authority to lay it down and the resurrection power of Christ to take it back up again. This is the destiny my heavenly Father has given me (see John 10:18). Whether I live or die is not important, for I know that IAM dispensable. To fulfill my calling in Christ, it is so important for me to imagine, believe, see and achieve the destiny my Lord Jesus Christ has commissioned to me (see Acts 20:24). When the Lord Jesus appeared to reveal my destiny to me, I stood up on my feet to be commissioned as His ambassador, to be a witness to what I have seen and to be All Things that He has revealed to me in His appearing (see Acts 26:16). God was delighted to give me birth by the truth of His infallible Word and to choose my destiny to become one of His favorite ones out of All Things in His creation (see James 1:8)!

I pray that Christ may work His perfection into every part of me. I ask that the Holy Spirit will give me all that I need to fulfill my destiny. And may He express through me all that is excellent and pleasing to Him through my life union with Jesus Christ, the anointed One, who is to receive All Things of glory forever and ever (see Hebrews 13:21)! In the matchless name of Jesus Christ, I pray. Amen!

About the Author

DR. BARBIE L. BREATHITT

DR. BARBIE BREATHITT is a certified prophetic life coach (AskBarbie.com), published best-selling author, dedicated educator and experienced revelatory teacher of the divine, supernatural manifestations of God, whose greatest desire is to see other reach, fullfill and enjoy their destiny in God. She is recognized around the world as a leading master dream analyst (DreamsDecoder.com) and healing evangelist with deliverance, signs, wonders and creative miracles following. Barbie's prophetic seer gifting and deep spiritual insights have helped and equipped thousands of people, including business, media and government leaders, and ministries in over 40 nations understand God's mystical ways.

Dr. Barbie Breathitt teaches individuals, trains corporate professionals and business teams, government leaders and churches how to recognize, respond to and release the activity of God with unique strategies. Her sincere pursuit of God's Kingdom and His eternal truth make Barbie's Texas-based Breath of the Spirit Ministries, Inc. a predominant worldwide foundation.

An experienced teacher, published author, prophetic voice, dream analyst and healing evangelist, she has released God's love, presence and breath in prisons, hospitals, streets, Europe, third-world nations, television, radio and the internet. Her deepest desire is to see people fulfill their unique destiny here on earth. Barbie's training, resources and personal ministry help others to interpret and apply the direction God gives them through encounters, dreams and visions.

Barbie Breathitt personally learned and now passionately teaches God's Love, Presence and Breath. Her astute prophetic voice and accurate dream analyses have blessed those in prisons, hospitals, Europe and third-world nations, enabling many hungry people to grow. Barbie has abandoned herself to the Holy Spirit with miracles, signs and wonders following. Many individuals have been miraculously healed in her meetings while others have experienced the Presence of the Spirit as never before. Her infectious humor promotes unity with those inside and outside the church walls.

An ordained healing evangelist, Barbie has ministered for over thirty-five years around the world. Barbie established and conducted three prophetic training centers. Barbie now lives in Texas and opened Breath of the Spirit Center of Training in 2004. Breath of the Spirit offers a variety of courses on Healing, Revelatory Gifts, Dream Interpretation and Evangelistic Outreaches.

SPEAKING ENGAGEMENTS

Traveling around the world to share wisdom and insights regarding sound, biblical dream interpretation, Barbie is available for conferences, teaching and hands-on training. Please contact Barbie's ministry at Breath of the Spirit Ministries, Inc. through email (info@DreamsDecoder.com), the website (DreamsDecoder.com) or by phone at (972) 253-6653 for more information.

IMAGINE: Believe, See and Achieve Your Destiny

The *IMAGINE* Series

Volume I will help you understand and fully comprehend that the Spirit of Christ dwells mightily within your sanctified imagination. Discover how to supplant the carnal mindset that has limited God and the displaying of His grandeur in your life. By resting in and experiencing the presence and glory of God, you will be empowered to receive and harness His truth, divine wisdom, revelation and supernatural faith to confidently realize, embrace and achieve your unique purpose and grand destiny in this new era!

God has given you a riveting new identity in this new era! Volume II inspires and imparts how to further unlock and mature your imagination to fulfill God's purposes for your life. Discover what it is and how to shed your worldly, carnal self—how to transition into your higher IAM state of being in Christ. Advance beyond the limitations of the third dimension, and gain supernatural knowledge of the mysterious workings of the unrestrictive, four-dimensional realm of the Spirit.

DreamsDecoder.com

The marvelous design and divine workings of the inspired imagination is further unveiled in this third volume. You will gain applicable spiritual understanding of how to access, unlock and interpret the meanings of visions and dreams that God skillfully fashions within your imagination. You will discover how to access your God-given authority. You will unite with the Fire of God to believe, see and prophesy in the NOW realm of God's faith. Through a broadened understanding of God's Word and clear spiritual insights into the profound power of imaginative prayer, you will be able to access the answers to your prayers that have been waiting on you to discover from the Genesis of creation. *IMAGINE* Volume III will equip and fully transition you into your new and glory-purposed identity in Christ. Your faith in God will explode into the supernatural faith of God!

In this instructive and illuminating volume, you will gain divine knowledge about the healing power of the subconscious, God's imaginative power and creative miracles. Volume IV will challenge what you believe, see and reason as truth and will help you identify the hindrances to having your prayers answered. God is restoring His people as One New Man! By using your sanctified imagination, you will discover how to come into agreement with God in order to effectively release your prophetic voice in this new era. You will obtain valuable instruction on how to increase, advance and prosper for God's kingdom purposes.

This fifth volume of the *IMAGINE* series brings the concepts learned in previous volumes full circle. Now that you have believed, beheld and obtained your new identity, you will discover the keys to successfully maintain that identity. You will encounter God's creative power, divine desire, godly disciplines of the imagination and lasting growth. The time to advance is NOW! Volume V delivers sound biblical teachings of how to use your creative imagination to release and prophesy into your God-ordained destiny and the destinies of nations. You will acquire the necessary knowledge and wisdom to effectively operate, persevere and prosper as a true Son of God and as One New Man.

IMAGINE: Believe, See and Achieve Your Destiny

DECODEMYDREAM.COM

ONLINE DREAM JOURNAL

Barbie Breathitt is excited that so many people in God's Kingdom are exploring the understanding of dreams. Barbie's 30 years of study and experience in biblically-based, spirit-led dream interpretation are available in an online learning experience.

DreamsDecoder.com and DecodeMyDream.com are our interactive web sites, impacting dreamers all over the world. We believe it is vitally important to record God-given dreams and to search out the messages they contain. The site provides a free online dream journal, dream evaluations, dream mapping, prophetic analysis and comprehensive dream certification training.

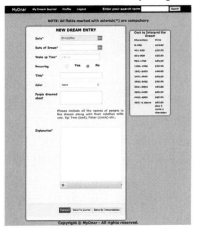

Sign up for your free online dream journal at DreamsDecoder.com. From the dream journal, you can easily submit your dreams for analysis by Barbie and our highly skilled dream analysts.

For additional resources by Dr. Barbie L. Breathitt, please visit
DreamsDecoder.com
Breath of the Spirit Ministries, Inc.
PO Box 1356 | Lake Dallas, TX 75065
(972) 253-6653

BOOKS

Dream Encounters–Seeing Your Destiny from God's Perspective is the "Rosetta Stone" to interpreting the illusive vapors of dreams. Uniquely inspired, and written to convince the greatest skeptics, and educate the most ardent believer, "Dream Encounters" will bring God's perspective, and understanding to the symbolic, visual, love letters, in the mysterious world of dreams. Take a journey into the sub–conscious night parables of the soul, to learn how dream truths impact your world; give direction, purpose, and destiny. Gain valuable keys to success by unlocking the mysteries of your dreams. Available as a paperback book, digital book or audio book.

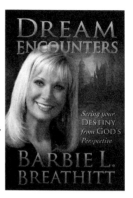

Gateway to the Seer Realm: Look Again to See Beyond the Natural is written by Dr. Barbie Breathitt a gifted Seer who has years of personal experience interpreting dreams and ministering in the prophetic realm. You will gain valuable insights into understanding the ways of God and the divine supernatural realms of vision, dreams, angels, healing and destiny. Open new dimensions of revelation knowledge to learn how to access the Seer realm through intimate daily communication with God.

Dream Seer: Searching for the Face of the Invisible is written by Dr. Barbie L. Breathitt to help the reader understand the Seer Realms of angels, divine visions, the voice and presence of the Lord and dimensions where the ethereal vapors of our dreams will become substantial presences when we believe that anything is possible with God. God is the giver of dreams. Jesus is also the Redeemer. So, like a knight in shining armor, He comes to restore the dreams we have allowed to fall by the wayside. The Holy Spirit inspires us to recall the images He sent long ago. God has mapped out our future. He brings the events of the world to bear on our individual

circumstances as He wills. When the events of our lives coincide with the correct timing of His plans, the next phase of our destiny ensues. The Holy Spirit knows the perfect time to bring the dreams and plans He has formulated to enable our purpose to come to pass.

There is only one right interpretation, God's. Every thing else is only shades of gray. Dream Interpreter will give you skill to correctly decipher the symbolism of your dreams. *Dream Interpreter* decodes symbols, types and shadows of images from a heavenly perspective in order to reveal the hidden mysteries that are contained within. Dream Interpreter will help the reader translate spiritual perceptions and happenings to accurately discern the events of the night. The gifted dream interpreter can decipher, convert and transform a concealed secret and then develop a blueprint for prosperity. You can learn to understand the evolution of vivid visions and dreams, the graphic picture language of nightmares and night terrors that come to visit and present truth about one's life. As a wise counsellor or life coach, dream interpreters fashion destiny bubbling up from the depths of the person's soul-potential to successfully guide the dreamer.

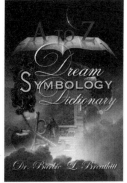

Acquiring a working knowledge of dream symbolism will enhance your ability to decipher the profound meanings of each symbol and then unlock the interpretation of every one of your dreams. Knowledge is power so learn to understand the mysteries that are hidden in your dreams. Their divine secrets will release your concealed potential so that you can design the destiny you have always longed for. Access the revelation knowledge stored in the pages of *A to Z Dream Symbology Dictionary*. Glean from ten thousand keywords and symbolic meanings that will inspire you to delve deeper into understanding why a certain animal, object, person, place, vehicle, article of clothing, tool, home, food, flower, weather pattern, action, emotion, color, or number appeared in your subconscious dream.

IMAGINE: Believe, See and Achieve Your Destiny

In her book, *Angels in God's Kingdom*, Dr. Barbie L. Breathitt propels readers beyond a natural understanding of the world around them to perceive and navigate the divine supernatural realms of the invisible world of angels. This one-of-a-kind comprehensive Biblical resource is full of progressive revelation and inspired spiritual truths. Dr. Barbie L. Breathitt covers fascinating topics detailing the origin, existence, and abode of angelic beings, their names, ministry functions, duties, and little known facts about the classifications of angels. She explores the nature of angels, the bold power of active faith and how the anointings of angels, seraphim, cherubim, heavenly creatures and host connect and guide us to and through the spirit world. Barbie shares her real life angelic encounters and the knowledge she has received through her diverse visitations, as well as her traumatic experience with the spirit of death. Discover the mystery of how recognizing the presence of powerful angels can redeem time when they are invited to step out of eternity to assist us in miracles, healing and deliverance. Learn how to prosper as the angels in God's Kingdom collide with the lawless evil forces of darkness and destruction. Gain spiritual understanding of how God's holy, intelligent angels clash with Satan's demons and diabolical fallen angels in today's modern world. Discover how the giants from the days of Noah are currently affecting society. And how we can defeat them through the blood of Jesus.

When Will My Dreams Come True? This handy booklet provides valuable detailed descriptions on dreams, visions and spiritual encounters. The information shared in these pages will educate the dreamer on the biblical techniques of dream interpretation. Through the study and application of the Hebrew alphabet and numbers, you will develop an Issachar anointing to discern the days, times and seasons of your dreams coming to pass. This collection of data research, priceless dream interpretation nuggets, gradient echelons of revelation, and prophetic vocabulary and terminology assembled in these pages will instruct

dreamers on how to record and accurately interpret the meaning of their dreams, so they can pray, decree and declare them into being.

DREAM SYMBOL CARDS

These artistically designed dream symbol cards enable the dreamer to tap into the hidden meanings of the symbols that appear in many dreams and visions. These cards are also useful in helping the believer decipher the symbolic language that God uses to communicate through the revelatory realm of the Spirit. "God is speaking powerfully through dreams in this hour. So many believers are having significant dreams but do not always understand the significance of the symbols within them. Barbie Breathitt has done a marvellous job of preparing dream cards as a tremendous tool to help this process. They are very high quality and fully laminated for long-term use. I was impressed when I saw them." Patricia King XP Ministries (xpministries.com).

Acquire all of Barbie's artistically designed, laminated Dream Encounter Symbols Cards. They are available as single dream cards, in an excel spreadsheet or in spiral-bound collections.

Dream Encounters Symbols Volume I features the original 23 dream cards starter set with 1433 unique symbol definitions which makes an excellent gift for those who have a desire to learn the meanings of their dreams. The collection includes Animals, Apparel & Clothing, Body Parts, Color, Color and Music Healing, Creatures Great, Creatures Small, God's Dream Language, Going Places, Going More Places, Home Furnishings, Jewels, Musical Instruments, Numbers, People, Seers' Word of Knowledge Ministry Card, Spiritual, More Spiritual, Tools, U. S. State, Vehicles, and Weather and Natural Elements.

Dream Encounters Symbols Volume II has 18 different dream cards with 619 different symbol definitions. The collection includes Birds (4 dream symbol cards containing a myriad of positive and negative winged creatures), Bugs and Insects (3 cards), Money and Finance, Nutrition (5 cards outlining the meaning of different foods, sweets, meats and vegetables), Plants and Flowers (4 cards detail what different floral arrangements and bouquets represent. God is giving His Bride flowers in her dream. What is He saying to you?), and Varied contains a list of Frequent Dream Symbols.

Dream Encounters Symbols Volume III has an additional 29 spiral bound dream cards that combines 913 symbols complied in helpful categories for ease of study and use. The collection includes, Body Parts (an extensive compilation of 5 dream symbol cards), Building, Rooms & Structures (4 cards), People (12 individual cards listing careers, professions and callings), Spiritual & Military Weapons of War (4 dream symbol cards describing the spiritual weapons of prayer available to believers), and Vehicles (4 dream symbol cards boats, ships, trucks, cars, vans, airplanes, rockets and more).

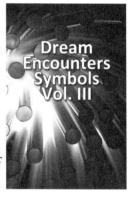

Action Symbols Volume IV, has 13 artistically designed spiral bound dream symbol cards with 386 different movements such as flying, running, transporting, and translating actions.

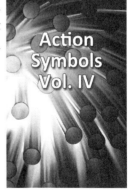

Dream Sexology has 4 unique and informative dream symbol cards with 95 unique symbol definitions that explain the meanings of your intimate naked dream language.

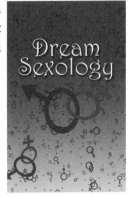

Sports & Recreation Dream Symbols contains 13 dream symbol cards full of 321 different hobbies, sports, games and much more to help you take an active part in the game of life instead of sitting on the sidelines observing the excitement of others.

TEACHING SERIES

The Dream Encounter MP3 Downloads and Manual is designed to teach, train, activate, and impart the skills to interpret and understand how God communicates to us through dreams and visions of the night. Jesus continues to teach through night parables, in other words, inspired dreams. The Bible gives us three keys that will be used in the end-time revival and outpouring of the Holy Spirit. The course topics include: Dreams, Visions, Transportations, Translations, Lucid Dreams, Colors, Numbers, Dream Symbols, Dream Interpretation, and Dream Teams and Outreaches.

The Revelatory Encounter MP3 Downloads and Manual is a prophetic course designed to teach, train, activate, and impart the ability to hear God's voice for yourself and others. This training helps you recognize and remove hindrances to hearing God's still, small voice. The course topics include: Developing Godly Character and Integrity, Old and New Testament Prophets, False Prophets, Immature Prophets, God's Friends, Knowing God's Voice, Difference between the Gift of Prophecy and the Prophetic Office, Forms of Revelation, Four Categories of Prophecy, Spirit of Prophecy, Nine Gifts of the Holy Spirit, Interpretation, Application, The Seer, The Watchmen, Intercession, Prayer, Intimacy, Spiritual Authority, and Developing Prophetic Ministry Teams.

The Angelic Encounter MP3 downloads and Manual is a course that establishes a biblical foundation for the proof and ministry of angels. Topics include: What are Angels? Ministry of Angels; Types, Functions, and Characteristics of Angels; Satan and Fallen Angels; and Angels and the Death of the Saints. Barbie shares personal experiences of angelic visitations from her life.

The Healing Encounter MP3 Downloads and Manual is designed to teach, train, activate and impart the belief, skills and abilities to move in the healing ministry. Topics include: Introduction to Healing; Jesus, the Healer; Issues of the Heart; Four Aspects of Healing; The Faith Realm; Take Your Authority; You Get What You Expect; Miracles Today; Hindrances to Miracles; Suffering in Regards to Healing; God's Voice of Healing; You Must See it to Be it!; Keep Your Healing; Healing Scriptures; Baptism with the Holy Spirit; and Walking in the Healing Ministry.

OTHER RESOURCES

The Hand Prayer Points Chart is a reference card that matches illnesses and diseases with prayer points on the hand. Great for intercessors who need clear direction for their prayers.

IMAGINE: Believe, See and Achieve Your Destiny

The Foot Prayer Points Chart is a reference card that matches the organs of the body, illnesses and diseases with prayer points on the foot. Great for intercessors who need clear direction for their prayers.

Healing Card is a reference card that matches illnesses and diseases with possible spiritual root causes. This Healing card is birthed from Barbie's ministry experiences and encounters of seasoned intercessors and those in healing ministries. Great for intercessors and individuals who need clear direction for their healing prayers.

Waking Words of Ancient Wisdom Make it a practice to notice the time on the digital clock as you awaken from a spiritually significant dream. The numbers displayed on the digital clock are often keys to help understand the message God is giving you in your dreams. Note the time on your clock, then look up the corresponding chapter and verse in the Bible. Allow the Holy Spirit to quicken the intended "Waking Words of Ancient Wisdom" to your heart and apply them in your life. This is a wonderful way to daily explore the Bible while you seek the deeper meanings of the treasures God is revealing to you through your dreams. Visit BarbieBreathitt.com to obtain detailed directions for use.

Dream Encounter Anointing Oil: Anoint yourself every night with this fragrant dream enhancing oil and pray for the Holy Spirit to visit you in your sleep. You will experience a heightened level of dreams, visions and visitations from the Spirit of God.